Crosscurrents/MODERN CRITIQUES

Harry T. Moore, *General Editor*

The Plays
of Sean O'Casey

Maureen Malone

WITH A PREFACE BY

Harry T. Moore

SOUTHERN ILLINOIS UNIVERSITY PRESS
Carbondale and Edwardsville

FEFFER & SIMONS, INC.
London and Amsterdam

For John and Mickey

Copyright © 1969, by Southern Illinois University Press
All rights reserved
Printed in the United States of America
Designed by Andor Braun
Standard Book Number 8093–0386–8
Library of Congress Catalog Card Number 69–11509

Preface

In the early 1920's, that remarkable figure Sean O'Casey came out of nowhere to have several plays he had written produced at the Abbey Theatre, among them three which have often been considered his finest: The Shadow of a Gunman, Juno and the Paycock, The Plough and the Stars. They were vitally Irish, tightly dramatic, and frequently comic in their projection of Dublin experience at the time of "the troubles." One group of Dubliners reacted violently against the third of those plays in 1926, and there were disturbances in the theater.

Two years later, O'Casey wrote an anti-war play, The Silver Tassie, which the Abbey rejected largely because one of its directors, William Butler Yeats, was against it. O'Casey was by that time living in England, where he spent the rest of his life. Many critics felt that O'Casey damaged himself by his uprooting: although he still wrote frequently about Ireland, his work, according to these commentators, lacked the fire which had blazed in the previously mentioned dramas, generally known as "the Big Three." Yet many of O'Casey's staunch admirers find greatness in the later work, which includes Purple Dust and Red Roses for Me. Whether such plays will take a place beside the earlier ones is a matter for time to settle.

Meanwhile, this hot Irish quarrel goes on, and we have O'Casey's dramas to read and, occasionally, to see (the Abbey eventually relented and added The Silver Tassie to its repertory). For augmentation we can go through O'Casey's rather uneven but fascinating six volumes of autobiographical narrative. And now we also have the present book, an extremely useful addition to the O'Casey literature, for it examines and explains much in the background of the plays which might otherwise be a puzzle to the average reader or theatergoer.

Outside of Ireland, only a few specialists in Celtic studies would genuinely understand the social and political origin of the central action in the O'Casey dramas. The Plough and the Stars, for example, takes place in Easter Week of 1916, and Maureen Malone shows exactly what that means in terms of the play. Similarly, Red Roses for Me concerns the Transport and General Workers' Trade Union Strike of 1913; this bit of history is also explained. But the author does more than merely explicate such matters; she relates them livingly to the plays in question, and in the process reveals a good deal about O'Casey's fundamental ideas and his skill as a dramatist. Her book is an extremely helpful guide to all readers of Sean O'Casey and a valuable contribution to the study of modern Irish literature.

HARRY T. MOORE

Southern Illinois University
March 2, 1969

Contents

Introduction

The purpose of the following discussion of Sean O'Casey's plays is to provide an examination of the political and sociological material from which he shaped them, making it thus possible to read the plays in the light of events and conditions prevailing at the time they were written. I also hope to discover by this examination what general conclusions may be drawn in regard to O'Casey's own aims and principles. I shall therefore pay special attention to the standpoint from which he views his material.

Two features emerge from this examination. The first is that whatever his material, O'Casey consistently views it from the standpoint of a defender of the working man. His subjects differ widely, but his theme remains the same. In the three plays dealing with Irish history, it is the common man rather than the Nationalists who receives his sympathy. In *The Silver Tassie* O'Casey emphasizes the sufferings of the common man in war with the same vigor as that with which, in *Within the Gates*, he exposes the exploitation of the common man in peacetime. In *The Star Turns Red* the playwright is concerned with the defense of Socialist ideology against the Fascist enemy. In *Purple Dust* he prophesies the victory of the worker against the "big houses," while in *Red*

Roses for Me he underlines the same theme in terms of the 1913 Dublin strike. His later plays on contemporary Ireland have in common with the rest a bitter denunciation of capitalist materialism. Whatever the period or subject, he views it from the same angle.

The second point which becomes apparent is his consistent defense of a highly personal creed which involves the worship of youth, sex, and art. The enemy of this creed, an enemy which threatens the spiritual life of the people just as capitalism threatens their physical well-being, is conventional, pietistic, and hypocritical religion. The conflict is emphasized in all the plays from *The Silver Tassie* on, reaching a climax in those dealing with contemporary Ireland. All this involves a scathing indictment of the Christian religion as now practised, particularly in the Catholic Church, which O'Casey regards as having aligned itself with capitalism and all the forces of pietism which oppose his most cherished ideals.

The three plays discussed in the first chapter were written in the following order: *The Shadow of a Gunman* (1923), *Juno and the Paycock* (1924), and *The Plough and the Stars* (1926). In order to give a clearer picture of the events on which they were based, I have taken them in the chronological order of their subject matter.

I should like to thank most sincerely Professor William Armstrong, who has revealed a capacity for inexhaustible patience in helping me with advice and comment. Also, my thanks go to Brother Anselm of Presentation College, San Fernando, Trinidad, who translated from the Gaelic the account of the raid mentioned in Chapter 2, and to the staff of Stevenage Library for their courtesy and helpfulness in obtaining books for me.

MAUREEN MALONE

Stevenage
October, 1968

The Plays of Sean O'Casey

1

The Rising

To understand the early plays which brought Sean O'Casey to the forefront of the Irish dramatic movement, we must examine the political forces which were at work in the Ireland of that time and which exploded in the events of 1916 and the subsequent civil war, providing the dramatist with the material for *The Shadow of a Gunman, Juno and the Paycock,* and *The Plough and the Stars.*

At the end of the nineteenth century, the political stage was commanded by Charles Stewart Parnell's great assault on the Act of Union, which had been passed in 1800, abolishing the Irish Parliament so that Ireland, with a minority in both houses at Westminster, had become politically impotent. Since that time the Irish had made many attempts, both constitutional and violent, at regaining at least a measure of freedom from the rule of Dublin Castle, seat of English government in Ireland. Parnell's constitutional methods were far more successful than those of his predecessor, Daniel O'Connell, since he held the casting vote between the two English parties and gave it to whichever promised to support the cause of Home Rule. He was also helped by the more violent action of Michael Davitt's Land League, which was independently conducting its own land war with the British government.

At the height of the great battle, which promised eventually to turn in his favor, Parnell, however, was forced to leave the political field because of the scandal of his liaison with the wife of one of his followers, and for some years the Irish cause seemed all but lost, with Ireland split dramatically between the pro- and anti-Parnellites. Hence attention turned temporarily from the political scene in Ireland and was directed to the appreciation and creation of Irish literature, which rose to prominence through the activities of William Butler Yeats and Lady Gregory during the beginning years of the century, while in the political field the mood of bitter disillusion continued. The name of Parnell achieved a fame comparable with that of Wolfe Tone in the minds of Irishmen and in the minds of many of O'Casey's characters, but the Irish parliamentary party took ten years to recover from the loss until, divided and leaderless, it was gathered together in 1900 by John Redmond.

As it became more and more remote from the realities of the situation in Ireland, however, two great organizations came into being, symptomatic of a feeling of national resurgence that was gradually taking place. In 1893 Douglas Hyde formed the Gaelic League, of which O'Casey was to become an enthusiastic member. This was a society for the furtherance of all things Irish, particularly the almost obsolete Irish language. Never explicitly a political movement, the League nevertheless gave such a stimulus to the rising tide of nationlism that many said it was the most strongly political of all.

The second movement to rise during this period was far less ambiguous in its nature. In 1905 Arthur Griffith formed the Sinn Fein movement, which, like the Gaelic League, was to go far in advance of the aims its founder set for it. Griffith's doctrine was not at first republican. It was based on the continued validity of the Renunciation Act (by which Protestant

volunteers in 1783 had secured a theoretically independent parliament under Henry Grattan), since he
regarded the Act of Union—which cancelled the Renunciation Act seventeen years later—as illegal. This
limited measure of independence was not now enough
to satisfy the growing hopes of such men as the young
O'Casey, who in the early years of the century began
to be in deadly earnest about freeing Ireland once and
for all from the connection with England against
which she had struggled since Strongbow had claimed
the kingdom of Leinster in 1170. The modest aims of
the early policy of the movement were soon to be
superseded by a more definitely republican policy, and
in 1910 Sinn Fein split into two groups. The old still
continued on its way, but eventually the new movement gained complete ascendancy. The older version
under Griffith's direction had kept up an unsympathetic attitude toward the labor movement, frowning
on strikes, and thus alienating those Nationalists who,
like O'Casey, felt their first loyalty was to the working
classes of the world rather than to all classes of the
Irish nation. The new Sinn Fein, preaching against
sweated labor and supporting strikers, went far toward
clearing up the suspicion which remained in those of
the labor movement who remembered the less sympathetic attitude of Griffith. Thus while attracting Nationalists such as Padraic Pearse and Thomas Mac-
Donagh, the movement was linked with Connolly's
Socialists and was at one with them in distrust of the
parliamentary party under John Redmond.

This distrust was not alleviated by Redmond's acceptance of a salary from the British government, in
defiance of the traditional practice of Irish members,
and by the approach of the Home Rule Bill (As-
quith's Government of Ireland Bill), which caused
violent reactions in two parties of completely opposite

views. Edward Carson, leader of the Northern Irish, prepared to resist with force any measure of separation from England, regarding the very minor measure of freedom offered by the bill as a threat to the dominant Protestant interests of Ulster. Meanwhile, on the other side, the aspirations of the Nationalists had grown far beyond so limited a concession. Attention focused more and more strongly on the rapidly developing Sinn Fein, which had become a symbol of Republican aspirations, drawing to its support hundreds of young Nationalists such as O'Casey. They gave every free moment that could be snatched from hard work and sleep and every spare halfpenny that could be wrung from meager wages to the cause that was sweeping up Irishmen of all classes to the crest of the great wave of enthusiasm that had grown with such momentum throughout the first years of the century.

The practical expression of this feeling was the founding of an armed body, the Irish Volunteers, an answer to the Ulster Volunteers of Carson. Meanwhile another armed group, the Irish Citizen Army, had been formed by James Larkin and James Connolly in defense of labor interests in Ireland. This body remained at first aloof from and to some extent hostile to Sinn Fein and the Volunteers because of class differences, since many of their members, including the secretary of the Citizen Army, Sean O'Casey, could not forget that the ranks of the Volunteers contained many of the employers who had tried to destroy the Irish labor movement in the great lockout strike of 1913. Moreover, the Volunteers themselves were soon to be split after the beginning of the war in 1914 by Redmond, who, having insisted on a measure of control in the body, offered its help to the British and indulged in vigorous recruiting. Those who followed him away from the original body became the

National Volunteers, the remainder under Eoin MacNeill retaining the original title.

Such was the state of things in Ireland during the first two years of the war, such the background for the Rising that had been in the minds of the leaders of the Irish Republican Brotherhood, inheritors of the old Fenian tradition of revolt at every suitable opportunity. "England's need is Ireland's opportunity" had been the policy behind all the blows struck against English rule in the past, and it was now once again to be put into practice. On Easter Monday, 1916, the Irish Nationalists under Padraic Pearse and James Connolly proclaimed an Irish Republic and seized the General Post Office in Dublin. It was the beginning of a brief struggle, whose end was hastened when the city was shelled by the gunboat "Helga" from the Liffey; the rebels surrendered on the following Thursday, having shown an extreme and tenacious gallantry amid the ruins of Dublin.

O'Casey set *The Plough and the Stars* against this background. He at once indicates that two bodies took part in the Rising by the words of the Figure in the Window, who addresses the soldiers of the Irish Volunteers and of the Citizen Army. Momentarily linked by hostility to England, they had (as we have seen) entirely different aims, the first being a purely Nationalist body, the second a labor force concerned with the struggle of the working class against the employers. Here O'Casey has a choice to make between, in his own words, the national tribe and the tribe of labor, and his choice of *The Plough and the Stars* (the symbol on the flag of the Citizen Army) as a title for his play indicates where his sympathy lay.

An additional significance is clearly intended by the symbolic nature of the flag's design, the stars representing the ideal, the plough the reality. The ideal which obsesses the patriots who took part in the Rising is the glorious vision of a free Ireland, achieved by the sacrifice of her people; the reality, the vanity of a few young men led by romantic dreams into a nightmare of bloodshed, while the common people, preoccupied with their poverty, stood by, apathetic or hostile. While he admired the desperate courage of the leaders, O'Casey refused to be swept away by their Nationalistic enthusiasm. His sympathy remained steadfastly with the slum dwellers of Dublin, whose sufferings were not to be cured by getting rid of the English. He never forgot that he was a Socialist before he was a Nationalist, and in one of his earliest publications, *The Story of the Irish Citizen Army*, he insists on the divergence between the Nationalist and Socialist groups which at times flamed out into open hostility before they finally joined forces in the Rising. It is significant that when he finally resigned his secretaryship through his disgust with Constance Markiewicz, who had a foot in both camps, he commented ironically that many no doubt preferred Cathleen ni Houlihan in respectable dress to a Cathleen in the garb of a working woman. It was thus, however, that O'Casey saw her, in the Bessies and Mrs. Gogans of the Dublin slums, unsentimental and deaf to the call of patriotism in the struggle to live. It is to them that his allegiance is given, rather than to the Nationalists, whom he satirizes as hotheads who are rushed into the fight through their vanity and emotionalism, only to discover the true horror of the violence when it is too late to turn back.

The conflict between the ideals of socialism and those of nationalism provides him with much opportunity for satire. His own views are voiced by the Covey, a Communist workman, while the Nationalist cause is satirized in the characters of Peter Flynn,

Clitheroe and Brennan of the Citizen Army, and Langon of the Irish Volunteers. This is not to say that the
Covey is the hero; he is in his own way as vain as the
Nationalists, and glibly parrots current rationalist doc-
trines in much the same way as the absurd Mullcanny
in *Red Roses for Me* and the Man with the Stick in
Within the Gates. Yet for all his intellectual vanity,
in his rejection of narrow patriotism he voices ideas
that O'Casey held deeply: "There's no such thing as
an Irishman, or an Englishman, or a German, or a
Turk; we're all only human bein's."

In Peter Flynn, O'Casey launches his attack on a
patriotism which is vain and superficial. The spectacle
of the self-importance which some men put on with a
fancy uniform always delighted him; later he was to
present us with the highly decorated Inspector Finglas
in *Red Roses for Me* and the elaborate rustic costumes of Stoke and Poges in *Purple Dust*. Peter
Flynn's patriotism consists in arraying himself in a
frilled shirt (compared on various occasions with a
shroud, a woman's petticoat, a lord mayor's night-
dress), white breeches, top boots, a green coat with
gold braid, a slouch hat with an ostrich plume, and a
sword which is "twiced too big for him."

The childish Peter is not the only Nationalist
whose vanity is satirized. The more lordly members of
the Irish Citizen Army are equally concerned with the
sartorial aspects of their rebellion. The handsome
dark-green uniforms were ordered by Captain White
of the Citizen Army (to the annoyance of O'Casey,
who was left with the more mundane task of raising
the money to pay for them), and the men eagerly
awaited their arrival. Since only fifty uniforms were
ordered, we may perhaps assume that those who wore
them were especially favored—the others wore bras-
sards of blue for the ranks, red for the officers. If this

assumption is correct, this would provide an additional reason for the pride of Clitheroe, who would stand at the door of his house, showing off his uniform "till the man came and put the street lights out on him." The whole notion of dressing their tiny force in readily identifiable uniforms struck O'Casey as pure lunacy. Far from securing treatment as belligerents waging war, they would be no more than decorated rebels, whereas in ordinary clothes they could slip out of any dangerous situation without being conspicuous. Brennan in the play discovers this truth and when the time comes quickly discards the uniform he was so proud of; he would never have escaped, he says, had he not changed his uniform for ordinary clothes. The vanity of Clitheroe and Brennan is also subtly mocked by their imposing military titles, as well as by their love of clothes; in civilian life the former was merely a bricklayer, Brennan a chicken butcher, a point which receives a gibe from Bessie during the course of the play, and O'Casey produces a sly irony from the contrast of glorified titles with humdrum trades. Absorbed in such trivia they are unaware of the practical realities and of the horror of violence, to which O'Casey had in vain tried to awaken his colleagues.

Yet his impatient criticism of their vanity and incompetence did not blind him to their true merits. For all their faults, they had in abundance the saving grace of courage; theirs, he says, "was a vanity that none could challenge, for it came from a group that was willing to sprinkle itself into oblivion that a change might be born in the long-settled thought of the people."

Among the other faults of the Nationalists, O'Casey stresses in his play their reckless indifference to human life. The Figure in the Window, in a speech culled from the various utterances of Padraic Pearse, emphasizes that bloodshed is a sanctifying thing, and several writers of the time reflect this reckless feeling. James Stephens admits that had freedom come to Ireland as a gift, such as is given away with a pound of tea, she would have accepted it with shamefacedness; the blood of brave men was needed to sanctify such an achievement. O'Casey's depiction of the heightened emotionalism of the characters in his play is an authentic reference to the temper of the times, yet he skillfully comments ironically upon all the grandiose sentiments as Fluther and Rosie stagger drunkenly out of the pub singing bawdily of the beginning of life, which, O'Casey seems to say, will continue, sturdy and vulgar, in spite of all the heady words of inflated patriots.

If, then, the leaders of the Rising provided him with ironic material in the contrast between their ideal conception of themselves and the reality of their vanity, impracticality, and emotionalism, the common people, too, are very different from the enthusiastic patriots envisaged by sentimental Nationalists. James Stephens, in his account of the Rising, *The Insurrection in Dublin*,[1] comments on the indifference of the man in the street to the great event. Many of these men, he says, did not care a rap which way it went and would have bet on the business as if it had been a horse race or a dog fight. O'Casey had much the same impression, evidently, for in the last act of the play he shows us Fluther and his friends gathered with equal indifference round a game of cards. Many, especially women like Bessie Burgess, who had relatives fighting for England at the front, were actively hostile, a fact from which O'Casey extracts full irony by juxtaposing the brass band playing a regiment to the boat on the way to the front with the departure of Brennan and Clitheroe to the meeting where they are incited to rise against Britain. So it is in the play that while the misguided but heroic Connolly and his followers go to their deaths, the common people seize the opportunity to pillage the deserted shops of the city. In his autobiography, *Mirror in My House*,[2] O'Casey describes the looters joyously collecting an assortment of articles, pianos, gramophones, and clothes, which they carefully tried on for size before carrying them off; and he presents much the same scene in the play, where Bessie Burgess and Jennie Gogan forget their quarrels as they return with a pram full of looted clothes, Bessie only regretting that she had not waited till she dressed herself from the skin out. These people are far from the ideal visualized by the unrealistic patriots, yet O'Casey regards them with compassion. He cannot blame them, for, as he has said, they were stretching out their hands for food, for color, for raiment, for life.

As well as being themselves unheroically indifferent to the great cause, they provide a mocking commentary on the burning enthusiasms of the patriots, in much the same way as Falstaff forms an ironic contrast to the high exploits of Harry and Hotspur. A patriotic song, "Dear Harp of My Country," becomes in the mouth of the Covey merely a means of "twarting" Peter; a patriotic slogan, "it's up to us all, anyway, to fight for our freedom," is merely for Rosie a useful bait to attract custom. In Act II O'Casey arranges a mock-heroic counterpoint to the high words of Brennan, Langon, and Clitheroe by juxtaposing them with the antics of the ordinary people. At the entrance of Peter and Fluther, who leave the meeting halfway through to come to the pub for a drink, their glowing expressions of emotion and their facile enthusiasms are a direct parody of the mesmerized state of Clitheroe and his comrades at the end of the act. The petty squabbles of Mrs. Gogan, Bessie, Peter, and the Covey are played against the theme of glorious war of which the Figure speaks, and their utter indifference to any such abstractions as freedom or integrity is underlined by the ease with which their rivalries are sunk in the common cause to loot as much as possible. The actual scenes witnessed by O'Casey, as well as his own dramatic instincts, dictated the irony which is the peculiar characteristic of this play.

The question of the autobiographical background of the play is in fact one of the most interesting aspects to be considered. Much of the material is taken directly from O'Casey's own experiences, described in his autobiography, and even when the incidents cannot be traced to this work, we are often reminded of their authenticity by a glance at the pamphlet mentioned earlier, *The Story of the Irish Citizen Army*. He tells us in the former of the rumors flying around to the effect that O'Connell Street was piled high with the dead, recalling Mrs. Gogan's similar impression that the Tommies were stretched in heaps around Nelson's Pillar; and he describes how his own mother narrowly escaped being shot, like Bessie, by a sniper. He, like Fluther and the rest, was herded with a crowd of others into a church, where he spent an uncomfortable night on a hard bench, and the next night he was marched to a granary where he found other prisoners whiling away the time, as Fluther had done, by playing cards. At last he was escorted home by a soldier who, shocked at the shortage of food in the house, demanded some from a nearby shop on O'Casey's behalf, reminding us of the kindly attitude of Corporal Stoddart. The creditable behavior of the Tommies is a point to which O'Casey was to return later.

It is from personal experience also that he draws the

pathetic figure of the consumptive girl, Mollser, Mrs. Gogan's daughter. She derives from a tenant of the room below his, described in the fourth book of the autobiography, *Inishfallen, Fare Thee Well.* Like Mollser, she coughs alone all night, unheard by her family, and her fate excites little sympathy—"Ow, is that all?" says Corporal Stoddart on hearing that Mollser died of consumption.

The picture of the dying child in the slum brings us back to the point that O'Casey, to whom such sights were all too familiar, never became hardened by familiarity with such horrors as many less sensitive people tend to do, and faithfully maintained his allegiance to the tribe of labor which set out to remedy a society which could take such things so casually. He indicates the miseries of those who live in the slums by a setting familiar to those who have read his two earlier plays, *The Shadow of a Gunman* and *Juno and the Paycock.* The tenement described here shares with the setting of these plays the distinction of once having been on a far higher social level than it at present occupies, consisting of the front and back drawing rooms of a fine old Georgian house. The lack of privacy endured by the occupants, one of the worst evils of tenement life, is immediately indicated by the intrusion of Mrs. Gogan into Nora's room and the later, more disturbing, appearance of Bessie, who frightens Nora with her threats. The description of Bessie's own room in Act IV gives us sufficient example of the squalor in which slum dwellers live, with its torn soiled wallpaper and its general air of destitution. The hardness of their lives is indicated by their apparent callousness to the death and disease which have become so familiar as to excite little comment.

Another social evil, prostitution, is touched upon by the character of Rosie, the girl in the pub. In *Juno and the Paycock* Mary asserted that her workmates went on strike because the employer's victim could not be let go on the streets, implying that such a consequence of dismissal was not unknown, and David Krause in his study of O'Casey claims that prostitution was a thriving and wide-open tourist industry in evidence on most of the main streets, despite the indignant protests of the first-night audience that such things were unknown in their Emerald Isle.

Thus the pressures of social squalor and the violence of the Nationalists alike bore hard upon the Dublin poor, and it is by the women of the slums that O'Casey sees the fight being most strongly waged against these threats to their lives. In the present case Nora is the chief representative of the qualities of steadfastness and protective courage which are peculiar to the heroines of many of O'Casey's plays. The room upon which she has imposed her personality is furnished in a way that suggests an attempt toward a finer expression of life, with its colorful furnishings and flowers. Like O'Casey, she loves pictures, and Giorgione's "Sleeping Venus," which hangs on her walls, may be reminiscent of the photograph of Thorwalsen's "Venus" which stood on the mantleshelf of his room since he could not afford a picture. She is particularly associated with domesticity, as her first action in the play is to set the table for tea, and it is to this that she automatically returns in her insanity. As the defender of the home she fills it with color and comfort and fights desperately against the violence with which it is threatened. O'Casey indicates this by the opening scene; the interior, strongly impressed by Nora's personality, the locks being strengthened to keep out violence and unpleasantness, is set against the significant sounds of men cheering as they go off to the political meeting. The patriotic emotionalism of the men is meaningless to Nora, who firmly places personal relationships before such intangibles as honor and freedom. Yet like Yeats' Deirdre she is helpless before the male fear of dishonor, which in effect is at the bottom of the hopeless but stubborn resistance of Clitheroe and his colleagues against impossible odds. O'Casey, too, regarded with horror the violation of personal relationships by the reckless pursuit of intangible ideals and indicates his feeling by the desolate scene at the end of Act I where the child Mollser, deserted by her mother, who has gone off to the meeting, creeps down to join Nora, whose husband has similarly departed. The disruption of all that is natural by political violence is frequently emphasized by O'Casey, here and elsewhere. While surrounded by natural scenes at the Irish Citizen Army camp at Croydon Park he had reflected upon the insignificance of all human effort contrasted with the works of nature, and upon the ugliness of a glistening rifle compared to one of the tiny daisies nearby. The same ironic purpose motivates the account of the young Republican's death contrasted with the courtship of the ducks in *Inishfallen, Fare Thee Well*, and also the idyllic love scene in the present play, where the natural images in Jack's song are abruptly terminated by Captain Brennan, whose success in detaching Jack from his wife indicates the power of the forces which threaten the home. Later the introduction of natural imagery in Nora's mad scene emphasizes the unnatural wreck of her mind by man-made violence.

The fight which Nora puts up against both social squalor and the violence which threatens her home is supported by the innate kindliness of the rough slum dwellers among whom she lives. Bessie, beneath her formidable exterior, is essentially kind, even to those from whom she is separated by political and religious convictions. Unlike the Nationalists she does not allow such considerations to override her basic humanity—she silently hands a glass of milk to the consumptive Mollser, seeks a doctor for Nora, and is finally killed in an effort to save the demented girl from the snipers' bullets. Fluther, too, exemplifies the kindly feeling which is typical of his class; he rescues Nora from the thick of the fighting and is commended by Mrs. Gogan for going around at the risk of his life settling the funeral arrangements after Mollser's death. He derives from an unknown figure whom O'Casey knew well and describes in *Inishfallen, Fare Thee Well*, treating the children with sweets and entertaining them in his sober moments with "Th' Wedding o' Glencree." These are the people whom O'Casey admires, fighting a far harder fight in their struggle against poverty than any of the idealistic Nationalists, who, though courageous, kept their heads among the stars so constantly that they saw nothing of the plough beneath. The *Plough and the Stars* thus shows its kinship with all the rest of O'Casey's work by asserting the primary importance of social issues and by revealing the lively compassion he felt for the sufferings of the class from which he himself rose.

2

The Terror

The Rising, as we have seen, was organized by a fairly small body of people and was received mainly with indifference or hostility by most of the people. However, after the executions of sixteen men who had taken a leading part, including people of such unquestionable integrity as Padraic Pearse and James Connolly, a wave of sympathy grew in force and intensity during the following years. English law was defied openly and in secret, while Sinn Fein maintained Irish law and Irish order by setting up its own courts, which left the English ones empty.

Finally, in 1919, the English resorted to terrorist methods and sent over a force of men left idle after their demobilization in 1918. Hastily equipped in a mixture of khaki and police uniforms, they were immediately nicknamed the Black and Tans, after the Scarteen hunt, a famous group of foxhounds. They quickly earned for themselves a notoriety that has lasted to the present day in Ireland. This notoriety, significantly, did not attach to the regular army (the Tommies) occupying Ireland at the time nor to the Royal Irish Constabulary, the Irish police force maintained by the British but chiefly composed of Irishmen. Yet another force in Ireland in those days was the Auxiliaries, ex-officers of the army, paid one pound a day, and neither amenable to trial by civil courts nor under military discipline. All these groups, the Tommies, the R.I.C., the Black and Tans, and the Auxiliaries are mentioned at one time or another by O'Casey in his plays or autobiography.

He has chosen a significant date for *The Shadow of a Gunman*: May, 1920. The struggle between the British and the Irish Nationalists had by that time reached its peak. Sinn Fein, the Irish Volunteers, and the Irish Citizen Army had been officially suppressed, and in March, 1920, a curfew (from midnight to 5:00 A.M.) had been imposed on Dublin; later this was changed to begin at 8:00 P.M. It was by no means an unnecessary measure, for troops and police, often armed with machine guns, would tear through the streets in armored lorries, shooting recklessly at people on the roads. Between January and June, thirteen unarmed people had been killed by indiscriminate firing by the Crown's forces, five had been deliberately killed by them, and a hundred and seventy-two persons wounded.

The most terrifying event, especially dreaded by the Dubliners, was a raid on their houses. At night search-lights played on housefronts, and the streets were filled with the rumble of lorries. If one of these stopped outside a house, the occupants would immediately run to open the door to prevent its being broken in; armed men would rush upstairs into every room, and any man found on the premises was in danger of being immediately shot. Those who were arrested were sometimes shot dead and reported as "shot while attempting to escape." Abundant references to the violence of the times are made by those who lived through them; O'Casey gives a graphic description of the armed lorries cruising through the streets and patrols creeping along every curb. His reminiscences are very close to the happenings which he portrays in *The Shadow of a Gunman*. That the contemporary references were a great attraction to the

audience for whom they were written is established by
Lady Gregory's remark that all the political points
were taken up with delight by a large audience. The
nervous comments of Davoren and Shields about the
recklessness of the Tommies and the sufferings of the
civilians would have been appreciated by those who
had personally experienced the situation. It is particularly significant that, as a rule, it is the Black and Tans
rather than the Tommies whom they fear; as in *The
Plough and the Stars*, O'Casey seems to imply that
the Tommies were not such bad fellows. He describes
a clash between these two quite distinct bodies in
Inishfallen, Fare Thee Well, when a British officer
saves him from molestation by a Tan and expresses his
contempt for them. Michael O'Maolain, a roommate
of O'Casey's at this period, also describes a Tommy as
expressing his willingness to be friendly with the Irish
people, and says that the British soldiers were not too
bad.

To counteract these forces, the now illegal Sinn
Fein increased its efforts to establish Irish law and
order in Ireland. These efforts were intensified in two
directions: first, the attempt to answer force with
force; second, the attempt to show that the Irish were
capable of self-government by setting up courts under
the auspices of the national body.

The Republican Army, of which Davoren was suspected of being a member, and of which Maguire
actually was a member, was a small but determined
force which achieved results by surprise attacks, by
ambushes such as those in which Maguire and Minnie
Powell were killed, and by the use of small mobile
groups armed with hand grenades. They operated in
small, flying columns of fifteen to thirty men, living in
concealment, sheltered and guarded by the people,
whose protective feeling is mirrored in the play by the

sympathy and admiration of the tenement dwellers for the supposed gunman and their anxiety to conceal his identity. The whole success of the movement was based on the support of the Minnie Powells and the Mrs. Hendersons, the ordinary civilians who had undergone a considerable change of heart since the Rising despite the many sufferings imposed on them by the long guerrilla war.

As a protection against the dangers of the conflict (and after the shooting of a policeman in February, 1920), the authorities imposed a curfew which continued until July, 1921. In his edition of Lady Gregory's *Journals*, Lennox Robinson described how the eight o'clock curfew closed the theater, and O'Casey gives a terrifying account of how he inadvertently found himself out in the streets when the curfew was in force. No longer able to endure the drunken behavior of his brother, O'Casey moved his belongings out of the house late at night. The streets were deserted except for two young men who slyly indicated that they had "a little sup in a bottle for th' Tans," and it was only then that he remembered how dangerous it was to be out at curfew time. As he stood hesitating, the ambush took place, and he departed as quickly as possible, knowing that it would be extremely difficult to persuade the Tans, if he were caught, that his business was none of theirs. Mr. Grigson's position, in the play, is equally dangerous, for he too is caught out after curfew, and his wife's anxiety is well founded, though O'Casey makes it ironically clear that her interest is mercenary rather than affectionate.

In addition to the activities of the guerrilla fighters of the Republican movement, efforts had been made to organize the Republic declared by Padraic Pearse and his followers in 1916. In 1918 the voters elected a large majority of Sinn Fein candidates (73 out of

106), and in January, 1919, the Dail Eireann, the Assembly of Ireland, was established and approved by the Irish people. This assembly proceeded to take over the reins of government insofar as possible, with the aim of rendering English rule in Ireland superfluous. The main feature of the policy was the judicial courts established to try cases which would normally come under English jurisdiction. Mr. Gallogher hopes that Davoren, the supposed gunman, will present his case against his unruly neighbors, pointing out that though he had taken out a summons against them from the British court before the Republican courts were established, he had not proceeded upon it as he had a "strong objection to foreign courts as such." This helps to underline the authenticity of the play, as the Republican courts had indeed come into existence early in 1920.

Apart from the activities of the British on the one hand and the Republicans on the other, certain other aspects of the contemporary scene are reflected in the play. The superficial nationalism which we saw exemplified by Peter and his friends at the inn in *The Plough and the Stars* is represented here by Tommy Owens, who sings patriotic songs and proclaims that he would die for Ireland, while quite ready to endanger his hero by vainglorious bragging in a public house. Minnie Powell, too, is enraptured with thoughts of Robert Emmet and other Irish heroes, yet it is her protective feeling for Davoren rather than any patriotic conviction that leads her to sacrifice her life.

Mrs. Henderson glibly quotes the Republican motto, "Sinn Fein Amhain," though her mind is on trivial local affairs rather than the great national aim. Seumas Shields is a professed ex-member of the Irish Republican Brotherhood and is full of current Nationalist slogans in a romantic, sentimental fashion, referring to Cathleen ni Houlihan, the Dark Rosaleen, and the Land of Saints and Scholars, though his patriotism does not extend to personal sacrifice.

Shields exemplifies another contemporary phenomenon, rising out of the activities of the Gaelic League. Throughout Ireland from the beginning of the century, a minor renaissance had swept over the country when, after the fall of Parnell, Nationalist feeling sought an outlet by encouraging Irish culture. In its wake came a wider appreciation of general literature and knowledge. Some of this obviously rubbed off on Shields. He is a man of much ignorance and superstition and little intelligence, yet he persistently reveals a knowledge of mythology, both Irish and classical, which would have been a closed book to a peddler twenty years before.

With Mr. Grigson we are presented with another feature of the contemporary scene; he is an Orangeman. The whole question of Protestant-Catholic antagonism reached a terrible climax at this time in the Belfast Pogroms, when, supported or ignored by the British authorities, the Unionists, or Orangemen, in Northern Ireland carried out persecutions of savage ferocity upon the Catholic minority, who fled south by the hundreds, and anti-Unionist feeling in the South was accordingly very keen. Therefore, the humiliation of the Protestant Unionist Mr. Grigson would have been particularly acceptable to the audience, for his bullying of his wife would be reminiscent of the bullying of the Catholics in the North, and in the play he is very effectively given a dose of his own medicine by the raiders. O'Casey raises this subject periodically in his plays, notably in the religious bigotry of Foster and Dowzard in *Red Roses for Me* and of Skerighan in *The Drums of Father Ned*.

One further subject remains in the consideration of

the play's adherence to historical truth. The raid which takes place at the end of the second act corresponds to an actual event in the author's life. In his autobiography O'Casey describes the intrusion of the Auxiliaries and his own terror, the temporary departure of the raiders, and the equally unnerving arrival of an attractive neighbor, Mrs. Ballynoy, who is in the process of seducing him when the Auxiliaries return; she runs back to her own room, narrowly escaping a compromising situation. Many points of this account coincide with the events of the play: the noise at the door, the terror of the occupants, the quoting of romantic poetry, which throws into relief the sordid surroundings, the discovery of bombs, an arrest, and the valiant cry of a prisoner who had previously been regarded by the other characters with little respect— Ballynoy, despised by his wife as ineffectual, Minnie, by Shields as insincere and superficial.

At first sight one might be tempted to assume that the play was based directly on experiences O'Casey later recounted in his autobiography, were it not that an article by Michael O'Maolain in the Gaelic magazine *Feasta* entitled "That Raid and All That" [1] gives an account which, because of the coincidence of several details, must be based on the same experience, although it differs in many respects from the more exciting version in the autobiography. O'Maolain was at the time O'Casey's roommate, and it was on Holy Thursday night that the house was raided by the Black and Tans. A young man wanted by the military, living in one of the two front rooms, escaped with the help of one Fred, who had sublet the room to him, down the passageway through a door and into the back yard. Fred was arrested and the house put under the supervision of the Black and Tans and the military. The landlord of the house arrived, and shortly afterwards his son was discovered in a shoemaking shop at the back of the house trying to conceal a quantity of ammunition and bombs—a regular arsenal, according to one of the soldiers. The young man and his father were placed against a wall as if they were about to be shot. The latter cried out, "We are Irishmen; shoot." Later, however, they were taken away in lorries.

It is difficult to say which of the two accounts, that in the autobiography, with the colorful Mrs. Ballynoy added for good measure, or that in the article, with the less glamorous O'Maolain as O'Casey's companion, is closer to the truth, but it is pretty clear that Shields and Davoren are portraits of, respectively, O'Maolain and O'Casey. They are respectively superstitious and rationalist in outlook. O'Maolain says of himself that he prays nightly; Shields is a daily communicant. Davoren's creed, on the contrary, like that of O'Casey, is aesthetic rather than religious. Like Shields, O'Maolain is a strong Gaelic Leaguer, and as such disapproves of O'Casey's gibes at certain upper-class Irish ladies who have adopted the current fashion of patriotism. O'Maolain regards himself as a "true Gael"; Seumas "could call himself as good a Gael as some of those that are knockin' about now." O'Maolain is something of a philistine; he regards the Abbey movement as an eccentric fringe of the Nationalist movement; Shields, we remember, has advised Davoren to give up poetry, though like O'Maolain he has read enough to make him fairly literate.

O'Casey in the same way would seem to have something in common with Davoren. He spent most of his time composing and reading sketches, O'Maolain says of his friend, and implies that a very early play, *The Crimson in the Tri-Colour*, was written while they were roommates. O'Casey, he says, would sing while he got breakfast ready; the play, *The Shadow of a*

Gunman, opens with Donal sitting at a table, singing. Twice O'Maolain asserts that O'Casey was regarded by his neighbors, unknown to himself, as a man on the run, for which reason they would do all kinds of errands for him—an obvious parallel to the helpful attitude of Davoren's neighbors. On the whole it would seem that O'Maolain's garrulous prose gives a fairly accurate account of the episode which was to become part of one of the best known of O'Casey's plays.

The social significance of the play is just as important as its historical aspects, and the locality is chosen with as much care as the date of the action. It is set in an existing district of Dublin, thinly veiled under the name of Hilljoy Square; the actual name of the place is Mountjoy Square. It is located in the northeast part of the city, not far from Dorset Street, where O'Casey spent his childhood, and just a short distance from the Gloucester Diamond, the public house which is the setting for the second act of *The Plough and the Stars.* Mr. Gallogher lives on St. Teresa Street nearby, within reach of the Coombe slum, where he works with a harness maker. The district consists of decaying Georgian houses which in the latter part of the nineteenth century were converted into tenements. Conditions there were bad enough for the careless and untidy Shields to write to the papers about the state of the yard. It was commonly acknowledged that these once-graceful residences of the wealthy, under the influence of the poor who found shelter in them, had become a byword as cradles of the lowest type of the city's outcast population. Like the tenement featured in *The Plough and the Stars,* the old house on Hilljoy Square had seen better days. Emphasis is ironically laid upon the once stately "Return Room" (or drawing room), now doing duty for Davoren and Seumas as bedroom, sitting room, dining room, and kitchen.

The irony is further underlined by the romantic songs and poetry of Donal, which serve the same purpose as the fresh, natural images of Clitheroe's song in *The Plough and the Stars*. The kitchen utensils, frequently mentioned in O'Casey's stage directions, are there as a sordid reminder of the composite nature of the room.

Among its other miseries, slum life inflicts upon its victims a degrading lack of privacy. Donal is pestered first by the entrance of Maguire, then Minnie, Mrs. Henderson, and Mr. Gallogher, just as Nora suffered from the intrusions of Bessie Burgess, Captain Boyle from those of Needle Nugent, Ayamonn Breydon from the constant interruptions of his neighbors, and O'Casey himself from the attentions of Mrs. Ballynoy.

Life in such places leaves its scars on those who live in them. Davoren bears on his body the marks of the struggle for existence, while Mrs. Grigson, in a phrase which brings to mind the dark masses of the slum dwellers in *Red Roses for Me*, is described as one of the cave dwellers of Dublin, the dimness of her abode having given her the habit of peering through half-closed eyes.

It is clear, then, that O'Casey has contrived to represent historical facts and geographical locations with considerable accuracy in the play, and yet by an adroit use of irony he offers us far more than a mere photographic account of the historical period. Like *The Plough and the Stars* and *Juno and the Paycock*, it has upon it the authentic stamp of the dramatist's creative imagination and, like them, is motivated chiefly by his sympathy with the poor and underprivileged slum dwellers of Dublin.

3

Civil War

As in *The Shadow of a Gunman,* O'Casey's choice of
a date for his play *Juno and the Paycock* was deliberate. It is set in 1922. At the close of the previous year
(December 6, 1921), the deputies appointed by Dail
Eireann to negotiate with Lloyd George had, without
reference to President de Valera, signed the treaty
that was to subject Ireland to the rule of the English
Crown and to accept partition as an alternative to
continued violence. The following year was to see the
full flowering of the seeds of violence thus sown. The
details of the conflict are not explicitly related in *Juno
and the Paycock,* but many points are touched on that
can be clarified by the events of the war, for the spirit
of bitterness peculiar to civil war is the spirit of the
play.

Early in January, the treaty was approved in the
Irish Parliament, with the result that De Valera resigned in favor of Arthur Griffith, who had been one
of the signers of the treaty. The change was paralleled
by a similar substitution in the Republican Army,
where Cathal Brugha, an opponent of the treaty, was
replaced by Richard Mulcahy. Dissension rose in both
bodies, and Griffith's summons to attend the "Southern Parliament" to approve the treaty and elect a
provisional government was ignored by those deputies
who opposed the treaty. The original Dail Eireann,
the government of the Republic which had been in
existence before the treaty, now continued side-by-side
with the provisional government created by the treaty

and supported by Britain; many ministers held office in both bodies.

The same duality was observable in the army, which, although still ostensibly a Republican army, had become an instrument of the provisional government, and gradually split between those who supported and those who opposed the treaty. The British troops, the Auxiliaries, and the Black and Tans were evacuated and the Royal Irish Constabulary was disbanded, to be replaced later by the Civic Guards, whose new uniforms, we remember, provided extra employment for Needle Nugent, Juno's neighbor.

De Valera, no longer president of the Republic, remained at the head of the anti-treaty faction and formed the political group Cummann na Poblachta, the Republican Party. Meanwhile, civil war became inevitable. The first clash came between pro- and anti-treaty troops at Limerick, the situation being relieved momentarily by negotiation by the leaders of both sides. Shortly afterward, however, the murder of the anti-Catholic Unionist leader, Sir James Craig, was used as an argument by Lloyd George to use more drastic measures against the Republicans, whom he held responsible. The combined arms of England and Ireland were in the hands of the Free Staters and directed against the Republicans. In a notable clash in the Four Courts in Dublin, Cathal Brugha, a man highly respected by both sides, was killed. Not since Easter, 1916, had such devastation been seen in Dublin, with three hundred killed and the east side of O'Connell Street in ruins. The Republicans were now known as diehards or irregulars, as they appear in the play. In August the last town held by them fell. Meanwhile two of the leaders of the Free State died: Arthur Griffith in a nursing home, of overstrain; Michael Collins in a Republican ambush.

The measures against the Republicans were in-

creased by both temporal and spiritual powers. The
Hierarchy of Bishops condemned them, while the government declared it to be an offense punishable by
death to be in possession of arms. Erskine Childers, a
well-known Republican leader, was taken and shot,
while four others were executed on the day of his
trial for the illegal possession of arms. The Free
State came officially into being on December 6, 1922,
exactly one year after the signing of the articles of
agreement, but the deaths went on.

Johnny Boyle, Juno's son, has been closely connected with the events sketched above. He was a
member of the boy scout organization, the Fianna
Eireann, which took part in the Easter Rising, and
later, though his mother begged him not to go against
the Free State, he took the side of the Republicans.
Now, for some reason not made clear, he has betrayed
a comrade, Robbie Tancred, whose consequent death
at the hands of the Free Staters is mentioned in the
first lines of the play, while at the end, Johnny's own
execution by his ex-comrades in revenge for his treach-
ery forms the culminating horror of Juno's tragedy.

O'Casey clearly shows in the play and the autobiography that he regards the killings of the civil war even
more senseless and criminal than the sacrifice of life in
the cause of patriotism as described in *The Plough
and the Stars*, with its unending chain of killings and
counter-killings, all to decide between two different
forms of government, the Free State and De Valera's
alternative to it, which in O'Casey's opinion were
practically indistinguishable. Seeing around him in
the slums the truly desperate problems of human suffering, forgotten in the futile conflict of meaningless
principles, he is totally impatient of the murderous
squabbling of both sides. "Still an' all he died a noble
death an' we'll bury him like a king," a neighbor says

of the dead Tancred. "An' I'll go on livin' like a pauper," replies his mother bitterly.

Lives were lavishly spent, and though O'Casey does not describe in his autobiography any specific incident on which the play was based, certain episodes are in spirit very relevant to the material of the play, emphasizing the sufferings of the common people in the needless civil war and the conditions in which they have to live. The pathetic incident of Mrs. Moore,[1] whose two sons and daughter are imprisoned, the latter's sweetheart mutilated just as Tancred was, is closely parallel to the situation in *Juno and the Paycock.* The sickening irony of an assumption of piety on the part of the murderers in this incident is reminiscent of the direction to Johnny Boyle, as he is taken out and shot, to bring his rosary beads, and we remember that Clitheroe was given a rosary by the friend who left him to die. The frequent association of death and rosary beads in the early plays adds a mocking twist to the theme, for the criminal violence is laid at the door of those who regard themselves as being "to God and Ireland true; for they still went to Mass, to confession and recited their rosaries ad lib." The sorrows of the old woman are thus similar to Mrs. Tancred's grief, and her death, alone on a country lane where she wanders, out of her mind, causes her husband as much grief as Mrs. Tancred feels for her son who lay stretched out on a lonely country lane, his head half hidden in a brook. As in *The Plough and the Stars,* the disruption of people's lives and the breaking of personal bonds by needless violence is regarded as a terrible thing.

The killing of comrade by comrade is also mirrored in *Inishfallen, Fare Thee Well,*[2] where O'Casey again describes an incident very close in spirit to that of *Juno and the Paycock.* In this case a young Republican is hunted down by an ex-comrade after having thrown a bomb into a Free State headquarters, and the cry of the young man echoes Johnny Boyle, who protests "are yous goin' to do in a comrade?" The relentless sternness of the Mobilizer reminds us of the similar fanaticism of Clitheroe, Brennan, and Langon. Johnny, having taken an oath of loyalty to the Republic, is irrevocably committed to the Republican cause.

A remark of O'Casey's tram conductor friend, a staunch Republican, immediately brings to mind the circumstances of Tancred's death. O'Casey describes, again in *Inishfallen, Fare Thee Well*,[3] how a friend rushes in with news of the death of one Captain Wogan, a Republican officer who had been taken out, killed, and mutilated in exactly the same way as Tancred, just beyond Finglas, a village four miles outside Dublin where Tancred of the play is said to have been found, and which was in fact the scene of many such violent incidents. O'Casey points out to his friend that "Wogan shot a man before he himself was shot," just as Tancred had been involved in the killing of the Free State son of his mother's neighbor, Mrs. Mannin, and once again we are reminded of the senseless series of reprisals which he regards with such horror.

Lady Gregory, also a horrified observer of the current scene, describes in her *Journals* how the Republicans had been shooting near her in revenge for the death of one of their number and also reports the funeral of the "poor Connemara boy who was shot," a lad of only twenty-two, whose grief-stricken mother and father followed the coffin.[4] The execution the previous year of four young Republicans, whose portraits and letters had recently been published in the Republican magazine, also strikes her as pitiful:

"They look so young and the letters to their mothers go to one's heart . . . And all for that wretched Oath." [5] The theme of killing and counter-killing for the sake of an abstract principle, the waste of young life and the sorrow of parents, is a fundamental theme of O'Casey's play.

A reading of the chapter "The Clergy Take a Hand," in *Inishfallen, Fare Thee Well,* leads to another point in consideration of the play. The conversation between O'Casey and his tram conductor friend is interesting in that, while the one is recounting the death of Captain Wogan and has no ears for anything but the Republican cause, O'Casey's mind is fixed upon the sufferings of the young consumptive girl who suggested to him the character of Mollser in *The Plough and the Stars.* The indifferent attitude of his patriotic friend is an implicit criticism of the mentality which can be absorbed in political questions to the exclusion of sympathy with human beings, and O'Casey's compassionate feeling for the "thin, frail hand, white as snow, clawing timidly at a brown blanket tumbled over the stretcher," [6] and his anger at the state of her room, where the floor of the bedroom had rotted under the oilcloth till the boards were of the texture of rain-soaked wallpaper, clearly show where his sympathy lies. As indicated in the section on *The Plough and the Stars,* he had little sympathy to spare for abstract ideals when he considered the more immediate social problems of ignorance, poverty, and disease which he saw around him.

The state of the houses in which people of Juno's class lived was, as we have seen, appalling. It is sufficient to quote Mr. Evans, C.E., who, valuing certain slum houses around this time, gave the opinion that the "Dyaks of Borneo live in palaces compared with these premises." [7] As in the two plays already discussed, the setting is a tenement in Dublin, poorly furnished, with the usual evidence, in the form of a bed, table, and kitchen utensils, that the room is used for a variety of purposes by the family of four people whose entire life is lived in two rooms. It is a typical Dublin tenement, near Henrietta Street, a semi-slum on the north side of the city and within reach of Henry Street.

As in the case of Mrs. Grigson and Davoren in *The Shadow of a Gunman*, O'Casey makes it clear that the characters in this play have suffered from the circumstances in which they live. Of Juno he says

> She is forty-five years of age, and twenty years ago must have been a pretty woman; but her face has now assumed that look which ultimately settles on the faces of the women of the working-class; a look of listless monotony and harassed anxiety, blending with an expression of mechanical resistance. Were circumstances favorable, she would be a handsome, active and clever woman.

In the light of these words it is interesting to read James Connolly's comments on a similar theme: "Upon woman, as the weaker vessel, and as the most untrained recruit, that struggle [for existence] was inevitably the most cruel." [8] Juno is a fair example of these words, supporting her family by working as a charwoman while struggling against the accumulated difficulties of poverty, misfortune, and a lazy husband. Like O'Casey's brothers and sister, she has potentialities that remain undeveloped through the conditions in which she lives—a waste of human talent which O'Casey regards as indeed tragic. Mary, too, shows signs of losing the battle against adverse circumstances.

> Two forces are working in her mind—one, through the circumstances of her life, pulling her back; the other,

through the influence of books she has read, pushing her forward. The opposing forces are apparent in her speech and her manners, both of which are degraded by her environment, and improved by her acquaintance —slight though it be—with literature.

The life of people such as Juno was a hand-to-mouth existence. Lady Gregory mentions the plight of a woman expected to support four children on less than twenty-one shillings a week. Heavy work was not difficult to find, and Boyle (like O'Casey in his early days, a builder's laborer) was out of a job principally through laziness; yet there was no guaranteed wage in such work as this, and money would come to an end with the job—we remember that the attraction of the job Boyle is offered is that it will last for some time. The docks offered employment to some, while other industries such as brewing (Guinness was a particularly good firm to work for), distilling, sweet drinks, matches, poplin, biscuit, and engineering factories absorbed many more.

The poor conditions and pay of the lower strata of the workers did not affect to such an extent the skilled artisans such as Jerry Devine. The social gap between these two quite different classes will be stressed again in the chapter on *Red Roses for Me*.

Teachers were still farther up the social scale, enjoying a very much higher status and comparatively high salary, being paid under the British educational system. Bentham would have had more to offer Mary than Jerry, with the additional attraction of his higher status, indicated by his "walkin' stick an' gloves" mentioned so bitterly by his rival, and the rest of his clothing—the brown coat, brown knee-breeches, gray stockings, brown sweater with a deep blue tie, all of which form a strong contrast with the famous moleskin trousers of the laborer Boyle.

Bentham's rival, Jerry Devine, is also significant in

reflecting a certain facet of the social scene. He is, O'Casey explicitly points out, a type of man becoming increasingly common in the labor movement, of "a mind knowing enough to make the mass of his associates, who know less, a power, and too little to broaden that power for the benefit of all." He presents, in other words, a criticism of organized labor. O'Casey, in his autobiography, voices significant disapproval of the development of the labor movement since the days of 1913, symbolized in his eyes by the change of headquarters from the old Liberty Hall to Parnell Square, since it became in the change respectable and ineffective under the leadership of William O'Brien after the departure of the fiery Jim Larkin for America.

> Official Labour had left the miry murkiness, full of the memorised shapes of battles, the shadow of which some day would take on the tougher glory of bronze remembrance, for grander quarters, where polished peace would have an easy-chair; gold-brown sherry would take the place of sombre, purplish beer; corduroy and moleskin be replaced by the natty dinner-jacket and the black bow. . . . The evening dress suit and the plus-four front of the Irish Labour movement.[9]

Jerry Devine, with his shallow principles which will not stand the test of reality, represents a party of men and women unworthy of the old ideals of the Labour Party and no longer truly representative of the working man, a party grown comfortable, fat, and inactive, divorced, as Jerry is, from the reality of human problems. O'Casey was to return to the point more emphatically in *The Star Turns Red*, in the presentation of Sheasker and his companions.

The activities of labor at this time are indicated by the fact that Mary is on strike—significantly a "sympathetic strike" characteristic of the early labor movement under Larkin, who introduced the technique of a whole group refraining from work in support of any one of their members whom they considered to be unfairly treated, in accordance with the slogan, "an injury to one is the concern of all." Mary makes her point clear when her mother taxes her with personal dislike of the girl whose dismissal caused the strike: "What's the use of belongin' to a Trades Union if you won't stand up for your principles? Why did they sack her? It was a clear case of victimization." To this her mother wryly retorts that "when the employers sacrifice wan victim, the Trades Unions go wan betther be sacrificin' a hundred." This brief conversation between Mary and her mother would bring to the mind of O'Casey's audience the whole troubled story of the long struggle between the employers and the workers which had flared up in the Transport and General Workers' Union strike nine years before the date of the present play, which, years later, O'Casey was to make the subject of another great drama, *Red Roses for Me.*

The first Irish Trades Union Congress took place in 1894. Thereafter the labor movement gathered strength under Jim Larkin, a popular orator and a great hero of O'Casey, and Jim Connolly, who aimed at uniting the two powerful movements of his day, labor and nationalism. In 1912 Connolly founded the Irish Labour Party, and the following year saw the great Transport and General Workers' Union strike mentioned above. The cause of Labor was for a time staggered by the failure of the strike, but revived gradually and strikes continued to take place. The hours of the workers were long, usually forty-eight hours a week, the pay ranging from £1 to £1 10s per week for older workers and less for young ones. The conditions of work were unsatisfactory, with primitive sanitary facilities and oppressive atmosphere. As Mary implies, some of the girls were driven to the streets to seek a better living, and the situation was a recognized cause of prostitution.

"Captain" Boyle and Joxer Daly touch upon another problem of Irish life, that of drinking. Their indulgence, like Boyle's fanciful dream of life at sea, is clearly based on a desire to escape from the harsh realities of the life around them, as is shown by Boyle's reaction to unpleasant news at the end of the play: "I'm goin' out now to have a few dhrinks with th' last few makes [sixpences] I have." In the light of these ideas it is interesting to consider the comment of a noted Irish social critic: "The Irishman . . . drinks to attain forgetfulness of the whole human condition—that condition to which he feels so exceedingly ill-adapted." [10] Certainly Boyle feels unable to cope with the problems his wife faces daily.

With Joxer, Boyle shows that the current development of culture and of emotional Nationalist feeling with which Davoren and Shields had been touched had permeated even to their low level, and their indulgence in outworn patriotic sayings and attitudes is part of the Walter Mitty-like dream which Boyle has created with himself as hero. Joxer, a past member of the National Foresters, sings an emotional ballad by Thomas Moore on the woes of Ireland, refers to "Napper Tandy" from "The Wearin' o' the Green," and his first choice of a song at the party is another patriotic ballad by Moore about the hero Robert Emmet. He has read a little, as his reference to a mysterious work, *Elizabeth, or the Exile of Siberia* shows, and he can quote from Newbolt. Boyle refers casually to Deirdre of the Sorrows, a tragic heroine of Irish mythology, applying the term more aptly than he knows to Juno, and grandly though inaccurately attempts to speak in Irish (genuine patriots speak it fluently, and only worthless pretenders use it as a social asset, according to O'Casey, and many a character is damned or blessed by his attitude to Gaelic, as in *The Drums of Father Ned* and elsewhere). Boyle composes spirited poetry on the topic of labor against employers, ironical in one so anxious to avoid any form of labor himself, though his true literary interests are not elevated; he criticizes Mary's reading of Ibsen's plays, the titles of which mislead him into thinking they are children's stories, and when Juno leaves he demands not the pious little *Irish Messenger*, a Catholic weekly pamphlet, but the seamy newspaper *News of the World*. Boyle's Irish culture is even more superficial than that of Shields or Tommy Owens, but like them he shows by the very fact that he has absorbed some of it how pervasive was the influence wielded by Hyde and the Gaelic League.

While he escapes, Juno remains grimly sober to deal with each problem as it arrives, bearing witness to O'Casey's view of women as a whole, outlined in a letter to me in January, 1959: "Women aren't nobler than men, but they are nearer to life, more enduring, and usually readier to face things and overcome bad times—though not all of them . . . they are often less selfish . . . they are nearer to the realities of life than men." Nora's child, though without a father, will have what's far better—it will have two mothers. Juno, like Nora and Minnie, fulfills the truth of these words, while the men are conspicuously weak and cowardly by contrast.

As in previous plays, the ugly man-made violence of contemporary events is contrasted with songs containing natural imagery. Boyle, when alone, sings of love, spring, and robins nesting; Mrs. Madigan at the

party recalls a pastoral scene similar to that recalled by
Jack and Nora, of two lovers in the countryside, and
sings of little green leaves, butterflies, and blackbirds.
Joxer's pathetic attempt at singing conveys similar
images—the mavis and the dewdrop on the rose. Mary
recalls a lecture given by Jerry on humanity's strife
with nature and quotes verses which describe the dual
nature of human life, which consists of ugliness as
well as beauty. That the ugliness is due to man is
made clear by Juno's remark, "These things have
nothin' to do with the Will o' God. Ah, what can
God do agen the stupidity o' men?"

Like the poor in *Red Roses for Me*, the characters
of the present play find solace for their hard life in
their religion, and references to Catholic worship are
sprinkled throughout the play; the mourners at the
funeral of Robbie Tancred sing a well-known Catholic hymn, while his mother and later Juno appeal to
the Sacred Heart and to the Virgin, both objects of
specifically Catholic worship. Johnny clings supersti-
tiously to the power of the lights in front of a picture
of the Virgin and the statue of St. Anthony; Boyle
mentions scornfully his wife's devotion to St. Anthony
and the Little Flower (St. Teresa), and his daughter
is a member of the devotional society, the Children of
Mary. She is tempted desperately to question the existence of God at the end of the play, but Juno
staunchly replies, "We'll want all the help we can get
from God an' His Blessed Mother now."

One further feature of the contemporary scene is
touched on in the comments of Boyle about the
clergy.

> The clergy always had too much power over the peo-
> ple in this unfortunate country . . . didn't they prevent
> the people in "'47" from seizin' the corn, an' they
> starvin'; didn't they down Parnell; didn't they say that

hell wasn't hot enough nor eternity long enough to punish the Fenians?

These grumbles arise at the present time from Boyle's grievance against the priest who had got him the job he had tried valiantly to avoid, but his sentiments were frequently heard in the mouths of many resentful of the Church's hostile attitude toward the Republicans. O'Casey's bitterness against clerical interference in politics and clerical lack of sympathy with the poor is merely hinted in the present play; it first comes into prominence in *Within the Gates* and from then on swells to be a major theme in all the following plays. Nevertheless in Boyle's ill-informed comments we have the seeds of what was to come later.

Juno and the Paycock concludes the group of three plays in which O'Casey expresses his view on the troubled political and social history of Ireland between 1916 and 1922. After the riotous scenes during the first production of *The Plough and the Stars*, when narrow-minded and bigoted audiences expressed a vehement disapproval of his honest treatment of the Rising, O'Casey left Ireland and turned his back upon local Irish politics in favor of the wider field of international affairs. But he did not do so before he had made clear in these three plays the position he was to maintain consistently throughout his future work: that his loyalty and support were given above all to the tribe of labor; and in the next group of plays, though the vision is wider, he defends the cause of the worker as wholeheartedly as ever.

4

The Great War

By the time his third important play was acted at the Abbey Theatre, O'Casey already had many reasons for feeling dissatisfied with all aspects of Irish life. He was disgusted with the easy subservience of the Irish to clerical domination; with the timidity of his sweetheart Nora, who, as a Catholic, distrusted his rationalist philosophy; with the petty snobbery of the middle class, newly risen to prominence with the birth of the Free State after the civil war; with the intellectual snobbery of those who gathered round Dublin's "gods and half-gods," Yeats and AE; and most of all with the narrow intolerance and stupidity of the Irish public which caused the uproar at the production of *The Plough and the Stars*. It was time for him to go.

In March, 1926, six weeks after the turbulent scenes during the first run of *The Plough and the Stars*, O'Casey learned that *Juno and the Paycock* had won him the Hawthornden Prize for the best work of the previous year by a new writer. He was invited to London to receive the hundred pounds prize money and, after a short return to Dublin to collect his belongings, he settled himself in a flat in London and started work on a new play.

The move from Ireland directed his attention away from internal Irish affairs to the wider horizon of world events, and the new play was to be the first of a series dealing with events which dominated the world scene between 1914 and 1945—the two world wars, the Depression, and the rise of the totalitarian states. O'Casey's hatred of violence had been demonstrated in the early plays, and in his new play he was concerned above all to reveal the sufferings of the ordinary soldier in a war waged principally for the benefit of a capitalist society. The new, wider themes of his next group of plays led him on naturally to a different dramatic technique from the realistic style of his earlier work. A comment of Winston Churchill may perhaps help us to understand why O'Casey so readily adopted expressionism as a means of communicating his ideas on these broader subjects: "As the ill-fated nations approached the verge, *the sinister machines of war began to develop their own momentum and eventually to take control themselves*" [my italics].[1]

Expressionism, as used by such German writers as Ernst Toller and Georg Kaiser, based on methods used at various times by Gerhardt Hauptmann, Frank Wedekind, and August Strindberg, involved not only the use of certain techniques but also the choice of certain themes, among them hatred of capitalist war, of industrialism, of loss of individual personality in a machine-like society. The development of the style was intimately bound up with the realization of the mechanistic nature of our civilization; the expressionist may stand aghast at the way the machine is gradually imposing itself on the living organism, or he may be enthusiastic about the machine; in either case he accepts its existence and endeavors to deal boldly with the problem it raises. O'Casey here is dealing with the machine of capitalist-inspired war rather than the machine of industrialism. He feels that the bodies of young soldiers are callously thrown into it. Many of the expressionist writers were Socialists by conviction and, while ready for the inevitable class battle, condemned the capitalist war and those who glorify the hideous realities of war with deceptive terms. It is interesting to note while considering O'Casey's debt to the expressionists that Toller wrote a play (*Hinkemann*) dealing with an ex-soldier, a representative type rather than an individual, who returns home sexually impotent and finds his wife in the arms of another man—a situation which has certain parallels with *The Silver Tassie*.

Thus O'Casey, tired of the realistic technique he had used in the three previous major plays, seeking for a new mode of expression, with the memory of the First World War still in his mind, and deeply convinced of the rightness of pacifism and socialism, turned to expressionism, which already had been successfully employed in the communication of such sentiments.

The development of the political convictions which link him with the expressionists becomes clear during the fourth volume of his autobiography, *Inishfallen, Fare Thee Well*. A growing disgust with the Irish Labour Party, too respectable under the comfortable leadership of William O'Brien to concern itself with the old militant ideals of Jim Larkin, led him to look to Russian communism as an ideal. He describes how he posted off complimentary copies of his plays with fervent good wishes and hailed the emergence of the victorous revolutionary forces of the Communists under the Red Star. He states bluntly that in politics he was a Communist, and says that he tried to explain the philosophy to Yeats shortly before the poet's death. Yet many of the ideas of the play can be traced to a source nearer home than Moscow—the writings of Jim Connolly. As a writer, it is true, O'Casey had nothing but contempt for the literary merits of the *Workers' Republic*, Connolly's newspaper, but the anti-war protests it invariably contained struck a sympathetic note in O'Casey's mind. The sentiments that "all warfare is barbaric," that "not more than a score of men in the various cabinets of the world have brought about this war," that "we see a small section of the possessing class prepared to launch two nations into war in order to maintain a *small portion* of their privileges," [2] are all in accord with the bitter ironies of *The Silver Tassie*.

From the first it becomes clear that the wealth of factual detail of contemporary life common to the first three plays is not to be found here. The period is fixed by a reference to the Battle of the Marne (September, 1914), the scene of the first act by the Irish accents of the characters and a reference to the Cross-Country Championship of County Dublin, won by Harry, while an occasional reference gives a very brief glimpse of life at the time: Jessie Taite is working on munitions, female labor being needed then as in 1940 to replace men drafted into the army; Susie Monican becomes a V.A.D. nurse, and the uniforms of the men and officers are of the 1914–18 period. Contrasted with the technique of the earlier plays, which involves continual references to contemporary life, these occasional indications of the contemporary scene are very slender. This meagerness of detail indicates that this is not a picture of the war in the same sense as R. C. Sherriff's *Journey's End* presented it, or in the sense that *Oak Leaves and Lavender* was to portray the Second World War. The subject is "war."

The first act places us in the same sordid, confined atmosphere of the working-class home we have experienced before. Yet it is not specifically an Irish home, not specifically a tenement—O'Casey is not about to present us with protest against the participation of the Irish in the war. Using a favorite device he indicates the main theme of the play by an object seen through a window; we can see the center mast of the steamer, indicating the approaching departure of the soldiers, just as the spire and chimneys are significantly visible in *The Star Turns Red* and as the railway signal is seen in *Red Roses for Me*.

The characters themselves give a hint of the new technique he is to use more fully in the second act, for they too have lost much of their individuality in comparison with the working-class people of the early plays. Simon and Sylvester have nothing of the idiosyncratic personalities of Boyle and Joxer, while Mrs. Foran and Mrs. Heegan are vague sketches compared to Juno and Bessie Burgess. The detailed lines of individuality in characters begin to pale from this play onwards until the creation of Brennan o' the Moor, so that while at a first glance similar to the earlier characters, Simon and Sylvester and their companions are significantly different, for they form a collective representation of the working class rather than so many highly individualized characters. Harry Heegan, like Barney and Teddy, is a "typical young worker," individualized only by his physical exuberance as Teddy is by his violence. He is singled out, not because of any distinguishing feature of personality, but because it is his fate to represent throughout the play the fate of the crippled war victims in general, and his physical vitality is emphasised only to strengthen the bitter contrast of what he was before the war with what he becomes afterwards.

The social implications of the setting are reminiscent of the early plays, emphasizing the depressing effects of poverty on the inmates of the slum. Mrs. Heegan is worn out by the hardships of her life; Mrs. Foran is "one of the many gay, careworn women of the working-class." Natural human relationships become soured or mercenary through the grinding effects of poverty; wives become overworked hags, husbands bullies or wastrels. In the present play, Mrs. Heegan's primary consideration is not her son's safety but the money she would lose if he were to desert, and having pushed her son into the hell of the second act, she sighs with unconscious irony, "Thanks be to Christ that we're after managin' to get the three of them away *safely*" [my italics].

But the souring of human relationships is merely one aspect of the main theme of the play, which is the exploitation of the workers in peace and war. The strength of Sylvester and Simon has been slowly drained by exploitation throughout their lives, the latter in particular suffering by the exploitation of his higher intelligence. Harry "isn't naturally stupid; it is the stupidity of persons in high places that has stupefied him." O'Casey has said much the same about the way in which social privilege took away the talents of his own gifted brothers and sister, whose abilities, unlike his own, were unable to overcome the oppressive conditions in which they lived.

Yet Harry is shown at the beginning as rich in many things. He has youth, health, strength, and vitality, consistently associated with bright colors such as the red and yellow which signify his exuberance. He is a worshipper of physical qualities, symbolized by the Tassie, sign of youth, strength, and victory, and he holds it aloft as a priest would elevate a chalice, though joyously rather than reverentially. He is the center of attention; two girls rival each other for his favor, and his attraction for both of them lies in his purely physical qualities. Having these, he feels no need for conventional riches. Teddy Foran, too, reveals his vitality in his brutal domination of his wife. They are two men overflowing with animal spirits; yet through the first scene, sinister hints of the fate that is to overtake them are unobtrusively inserted into the general pattern of rejoicing. Sylvester and Simon discuss Harry's legendary prowess in past events; but in the background Susie indicates his future by polishing the rifle ready for his return to the front. With careless indifference, Harry himself reminds us of the harsh realities of war in his casual reference to the "little Jock we left shrivellin' on the wire after the last push." In the last attempt to continue the excitement they are never to enjoy again he suggests that they should stay behind for a party, but the combined voices of relations and neighbors thrust them forward.

In his autobiography O'Casey more than once speaks with bitterness of the death of the young in war, and treats with fierce sarcasm the conventional attitude that it is glorious, an attitude he regards as the whining heresy of old age. It is with this feeling that he conveys the extreme sufferings of the young soldiers in the second act. As we have seen, it is the problem of war, rather than individuals, with which he is dealing, and were he to do this in the style, for instance of *Journey's End*, or to follow the commercially safer paths of realism, our attentions would be riveted on the single hero and the breadth of effect be lost. Harry, in this act, disappears into the general melting pot of war. The soldiers are no longer individuals—they are merely first, second, third, and fourth, each with identical sufferings, fears, and hopes. They enter in a close mass, as if each were keeping the other from falling, utterly weary. They should appear, O'Casey says, as if locked together. They are an inextricable mass of humanity. Of all the principal characters, only Barney remains to carry on the continuity through the distorted hell of the second act to the normal world of Acts III and IV.

The soldiers are taking part in the Battle of the

Marne and must be somewhere along the battlefront of two hundred miles between Paris and Verdun. They have been there, it seems to them, for an interminable length of time, and they feel that they have been forgotten. Winston Churchill observed that this feeling of weary inactivity was a feature of this phase of the war, where along the great battlefront the weary troops were in loose, desperate conflict: "Then all of a sudden one side sustained the impression that it was the weaker, and that it had had the worst of it."[3]

The monotony of the soldiers' lives was not the least feature of their torment. Yet men were dying all the time, young men fighting other young men whom they neither knew nor hated, and much of O'Casey's bitterness rose from the feeling that the working-class soldiers of the British Army owed their allegiance to their comrade workers on the other side, rather than to the capitalists to whose advantage their blood was being spilt. The old choice between rival allegiances is once again made in the same way; patriotic obligations take second place to loyalty to class, for O'Casey stood "under a red flag rather than the green banner"[4]— certainly not under a Union Jack. Later, an apparent inconsistency is to appear in his attitude when he seems to throw in his lot with Britain and applaud the heroic death of young pilots in the Battle of Britain in *Oak Leaves and Lavender,* yet when we remember that the 1940 conflict was against the enemy of communism, we can understand more clearly why O'Casey uneasily put aside his deep-rooted pacifist convictions.

The chief question of the second act is voiced by the First Soldier, "Wy'r we 'ere?" In turn, answers are sought from those who ought to know, and in turn we see the pathetic inadequacy of their answers. Religion supplies complacent patriotic platitudes, families are merely interested in getting the separation money, and the men's ignorance of the cause of their plight gives their situation an additional pathos. They are uneducated men, directed in all their doings by those in authority; told to fight, they have no choice, told to vote they do so unthinkingly, for "Harry has gone to the trenches as unthinkingly as he would go to a polling booth." To the questions of the helpless men, those who should know are unable to supply the answer, or else the answer, that of the wanton destruction of human life for economic purposes, is too terrible to contemplate. When they are dead, but not till then, they may understand it all.

The privileged classes, who save their own skins while giving pep talks to the soldiers, are represented with savage satire. The civilian Visitor, with his portly, rubicund face, who "sees only the arses of the guns," who is careful to obey all the safety regulations while protesting against their restrictions, is exposed with sardonic humor. His class is indicated by the educated manner of his speech, contrasting with the carefully emphasized cockney of the soldiers. He takes a serious view of Barney's misdemeanor of a cock filched from a nearby café, or estaminet, for a cock's life, unlike that of the soldiers, apparently, is sacred.

The "Brass-hat" responsible for Barney's capture is similarly viewed with clearsighted honesty by the soldiers. In a formalized list of questions they stress the fact that he eats, sleeps, and whores well, but as to fighting, "Napoo; 'e 'as to do the thinking for the Tommies." He is another of the privileged class whose privileges extend to the daughter of the local landlord while the Tommy is punished for his attempt on the landlord's poultry. His war efforts amount to the voicing of encouraging sentiments, ironically echoed by the stretcher bearers.

The Staff-Wallah similarly is an object of satire. He enters with a springing hop to enunciate some new trifling regulation or to announce some compulsory dreary lecture for the entertainment of the troops before he goes back to his more lively entertainments at his hotel.

As a final jab of irony, a quick reminder of the days of Harry's football triumphs comes into the midst of the destruction—a ball, in Harry's colors of red and yellow sent by a girl friend to the Second Soldier to "play your way . . . over the top," indicating how far from understanding their sufferings the people safe at home are, and how far from play is the business in which these soldiers are involved.

As the first act is devoted to showing the wealth of physical attributes of youth and the glorious animal vitality later to be squandered, the second act, then, asks why this should be and who is responsible for the waste. The answer also is given here—the privileged classes who, while hypocritically professing Christianity, want war for their own reasons; they force the soldiers into it while remaining safe themselves, and they have no comprehension of the sacredness of human life. Act III deals with another question: What help can these victims of society hope for from society when they have made their sacrifice? The answer is given in the last two acts; they are beyond help from friends, from medical science, from religion. By natural law life goes on, and the half-dead are outcasts.

The characters of the first act gather round Harry in the hospital in an embarrassed effort to bring him consolation for his shattered limbs. Their well-meant words only add to his agony. His mother is still thinking of the financial side of it, Jessie will have nothing to do with him, Susie regards him with indifferent pity. Medicine, in the person of Surgeon Maxwell, is as careless of his misery as of the trivial indisposition of Sylvester—his case is all too common. As a last hope he turns to religion, but conventional religion is powerless against the economic forces which thrust society into war; calm and dignified, the Sister of the nursing order goes out to join a prayer to the Mother of Mercy, but Harry's despairing cry, "God of the miracles, give a poor devil a chance," remains unheard.

The fourth act shows the hopelessness of Harry's life now that he is a cripple. Barney takes his place in the affections of Jessie, and his life has become a meaningless "tinkle, tinkle in the nighttime." Teddy, now helpless through his blindness, is dependent on the wife he bullied. Together the two men take leave of all that is best in a life which now has no place for them. The survivors carry on, enjoying the dance of life to the full. They are not cruel—life cannot stand still; as Susie points out, "We, who have come through the fire unharmed, must go on living." O'Casey withholds from society, guilty of these crimes, any salve to conscience in the thought that its victims can be comfortably rehabilitated. He forces us to see that there is no hope for those mutilated in war. His attitude is as uncompromising as that of Shaw to poverty; society must not be allowed the luxury of conscience money in the form of gifts to charity or sympathy with war victims; this is mere patching up. It is the cause which both writers attack—poverty must go; war must cease.

While these themes are central to the play, another of equal importance is raised, that of the irony of Christian states at war. Winston Churchill in *The World Crisis* shows that he too appreciated this irony: "Torture and Cannibalism were the only two expedients that the civilized, scientific, Christian States had been able to deny themselves: and these were of doubtful utility." [5] At the time of its first production, the play was fiercely resented as a mockery of religion because of the liturgical nature of the second act, which depicts the soldiers worshipping the gun as their savior. The point O'Casey wished to make was a bitter criticism, of society, not of religion. Christianity is the accepted religion of Western society, and one of its main tenets is thou shalt not kill. Yet although society gives mouth honor to established religion and though its members are nominally Christian, it flagrantly ignores the basic Christian principles wherever convenient. O'Casey is pointing out that Christ-worshippers are in actual fact gun-worshippers, whatever they may state to the contrary—that the gun rather than Christ is the moving force in society today.

In the first act we are given a sight of the emptiness of religious professions by the sanctimoniousness of Susie. She uses it merely as a retreat from her unsuccessful love of Harry, and as soon as her attachment is broken and a new interest formed, we hear no more of her exaggerated piety. The ironic association between war and religion is also pointed out by Susie; she chants extracts from the Bible as she polishes a rifle and a steel helmet. Her mouth is busy with religion, but it is her hands that are busy with the reality. We are reminded once again of a symbol used in the early plays, the rosary twisted round a gun. Her violent, bludgeoning methods show that a religion of peace is not always spread with peace. Society would keep its religion and its actual deeds in separate compartments; it is O'Casey's opening up of the compartments and his showing of the incongruities therein that shocked his critics. Susie unwittingly indicates society's true beliefs when she equates God and guns.

"The men that go with the guns are going with God."

In Act II the religious theme is taken up in earnest; the Croucher's dreadful intoning takes on a far more sinister aspect than Susie's earlier sermonizing. The association of death and religion is continued as soon as the act opens. The fearful irony of the Kyrie Eleison, a prayer for mercy, is intermingled with the drowsy monotony of the skeletal Croucher.

The Visitor, as a representative of society, approves of religion as a convenient soporific for the soldiers; it "gives 'em peace," as he says with unconscious irony. The collapse of conventional religion is conveyed by the devastation of the monastery, while the half-dislodged figure of the Prince of Peace hangs over all, helpless and unregarded. The soldiers, it is true, retain enough superstitious veneration to prevent the Visitor from striking a match on the arm of the cross, an indication of his own basic insincerity; but when the hour comes they know what it is will protect them, and in what they must put their trust. They remember the promise made on the Mount that every sparrow should be cared for, but the implication of the play is that the "Estaminay cock" is more sacred than they.

The criticism is not, then, of religion itself. It is man in society that wreaks havoc on his fellowmen in the midst of peaceful nature. "What can God do agen the stupidity o' man?" asks Juno, and O'Casey, with his image of a heart-sickened God beholding the blood dance of his self-slaying children, drives home the point in terrible language.

Society's dealings with the masses whom it exploits in peacetime and slaughters in war, and its hypocritical profession of adherence to a religion which in practice it ignores, together embody the theme of this play, which is admirably suited to the expressionistic techniques which O'Casey uses here for the first time. His next play once again deals with the sufferings of the ordinary man and woman in contemporary society, this time in a period of peace. The call of the tribe of labor is still heard above all others.

5

The Depression

The Silver Tassie, dealing with the subject of international war, opened in London in October, 1929; a few weeks later the stock market crash brought economic disaster, and in the ensuing depression millions suffered ruin and hardship. Bankrupts committed suicide, and processions of unemployed became a common sight in the big cities of the world. It was from this material that O'Casey, with his eyes still on the international scene, formed his next play, *Within the Gates*.

Originally given the title of *The Green Gates*, it was to be a "design of Morning, Noon, Evening, and Night . . . [he] had thought of the play as a film of Hyde Park . . . geometrical and emotional, the emotion of the living characters to be shown against their own patterns and the patterns of the Park." [1] The fact that he had thought of the play as a film, together with the formality implied in the word "pattern," indicates that he was to continue experimenting with the expressionistic technique he had used successfully in his previous play. Many of the expressionists had been tempted to a combination of film and play technique, while the tendency to formal representation of abstractions rather than characters, common among expressionist writers, is a useful expedient in creating a pattern. As before, however, his bond with the expressionist writers is above all one of subject matter, for he shares with them and expresses in the present play a sympathy for the masses.

The new technique, dealing as before with general themes, strips the play even more completely of any very definite references to specific time and place, so that while we are reminded of the period of the play by suggestions such as the procession of the Down-and-Out and by occasional topical references, such as that of the Attendants to the gold standard, the connection between the play and the times in which it is assumed to take place is far more general than in any previous work.

The theme is parallel to that of the previous play in a significant way. As *The Silver Tassie* depicted the threat of war to the life of the body, here O'Casey is concerned with the threat of moral and spiritual decay to the life of the soul. Figures of death dominate the opening of the play; the statue of the steel-helmeted soldier, a war memorial, immediately recalls for us the war which had destroyed life on such a great scale, as is indicated by the skeleton-like hands of the figure which grasp the butt end of the rifle. The point is further emphasized by the information that the Young Woman's stepfather had died in the war, and by the Old Woman's offering of a wreath, which she lays at the foot of the memorial in honor of the forgotten heroes of the war, emphasizing the futility of their sacrifice. A connection between the physical deaths of the war and the spiritual death facing England is made by the khaki color of the Attendants, who are truly dead in spirit and also ripe for physical death. The young have been killed in the war along with all the vigorous qualities that made them great; "the golden infancy of England's life is tarnishing now in the bellies of the worms," the Old Woman says, and she repeats the idea more than once. Sycophantic worship of riches, trite, meaningless religion which bolsters up a decaying society, unwholesome interest in sensational scandal, mean snobbery, stupidity, hypocrisy, littleness of soul—these, rather than the guns are the dangers with which the young are faced. The band in the park plays "Land of Hope and Glory," but significantly it fades as the curtain rises, and the satirical intent becomes clear as the older Attendant informs us that "there's not much of the glory left, en' none of the 'ope."

Earlier he remarks that he has been listening to a pageant of England on the radio which made him proud to be an Englishman. That this is intended to be a satirical reference is made clear by a glance at *The Green Crow*, a pungent selection of O'Casey's critical and other writings.[2] Here he directs a thunderous attack on the fatuous drama of Noel Coward, then immensely popular, advertized by the fulsome praises of James Agate. Among other targets, he takes particular aim at Coward's *Cavalcade*, a sickly patriotic chronical which, ignoring the realities of hunger and misery, bankruptcy and unemployment of the contemporary scene, blandly progressed to a triumphant close, after which the author in a curtain speech expressed the hope that it had made them all feel it was "still a pretty exciting thing to be English." With the Attendant's reference, we are made to face the unpleasant truth that many Englishmen, faced with the miseries of unemployment, were at the time anything but excited. The fact is pressed home by the sinister march throughout the play of the Down-and-Out. The Attendant has just finished explaining to his companion the significance of Drake's Drum, which beats to warn England in time of danger, when a muffled drum is in fact heard—not the rousing tattoo of a great hero, but the mournful drumbeat of the Down-and-Out. Though they are reminiscent of the dreary processions of the unemployed at the time, for whom the phrase was currently used, the Dreamer points out that they are not the financially impoverished, but the timid thinkers and pessimists who "whine through to-day and dread to-morrow"—the morally down-and-out.

The pattern which O'Casey has drawn includes many sections of society. The upper class is represented by the snobbish Nursemaids in charge of the countess' baby, which receives much attention from the sycophantic Attendants. As soon as any disturbance starts, they are carefully escorted out of danger by the Policewoman, a representative of authority, who is eagerly submissive to those of high rank, such as the Bishop, and a staunch upholder of Mrs. Grundy. The lower class is represented by the squabbling, would-be philosophers who provide much of the humor of the play, for O'Casey delights in futile disputes of the sort they indulge in, where neither side is equipped to deal with the immense problems they toss around so lightly; and, as has been shown, he is not always on the side of the rationalist in the dispute. At one point the Guardsman joins in, but is baffled by one of the rationalists, displaying a stupidity which indicates that O'Casey was not one of the foolish socialists who imagines every working man to be a pattern of all the virtues. The soldier's participation in the dispute leads his sweetheart to point out that he, as a soldier, should not argue; a soldier's job, she implies with unconscious irony, is not to think but unthinkingly to act as a weapon in the hands of the politicians who do his thinking for him. In this case his job is "holdin' dahn Africar en' Indiar, en' teachin' 'en 'ow too behive theirselves proper"—a quick gibe at Imperialism, echoed by the Old Woman, who sardonically addresses the sister of the Bishop as "mem pukka memsahib."

A side blow at sensational and superficial popular

journalism, such as that of the *Daily Express*, is aimed in the reading matter of the four men, dealing with Murder, Rape, Suicide, and Divorce, from which they read salacious extracts with unwholesome delight. The Young Woman attracts their attention for a moment by dancing, and as she does so bitterly castigates their lechery.

Few of the lower-class characters are admirable in this play—the decaying attendants who have lost all healthy vitality of mind (except when they evince a momentary carnal enthusiasm for the Young Woman), the squabbling Men who dispute great matters with little knowledge and read the gutter press, the snobbish Nursemaids, hangers-on of the aristocracy, and the stupid Guardsman, ignorantly supporting the British Empire—all are held up for our disapproval.

The sufferings of the lower class are depicted in the Young Woman. Her unfortunate start in life as the illegitimate daughter of the Bishop and the Old Woman, her education by nuns who terrified her as a child with stories of hell, and her unhappy homelife all conspire to place her in her present position. Her attempts to earn a living honestly have been prevented by the manager's treatment of the girls employed in the shop; she prefers outright prostitution. Society has made her what she is, and now, as she appeals in turn to the Atheist, the Gardener, and the Bishop, there is nowhere she can find help. Only the Dreamer offers her, not security, but a life fully and recklessly lived and enjoyed.

The reality of her sufferings is contrasted with the deplorably impractical approach of the Bishop, who is wholly out of touch with real life. He is the representative of respectable religion, satirized before by O'Casey in his autobiography, where he describes the

Christ of the rich and powerful in morning suit, top hat, gold cufflinks, and diamond studs, with a neatly rolled umbrella in lieu of a cross, a similar picture to that drawn by the Young Woman, who accuses the Bishop of worshipping a Christ who wears a bowler hat, twiddles his lavender gloves, and sends out gilt-edged cards of thanks to callers.

Though anxious to show everyone he meets that he is an up-to-the-minute clergyman, the Bishop is in fact, behind his pretense of cheery broadmindedness, a fake. The unreal sentiments latent in the faith he represents are indicated by his rhapsodic praise of the "brave little birds," a sentimental attitude which indicates that O'Casey is still thinking of how far the practice of society is from the principles of the Sermon on the Mount, which promises that human good shall be considered even more than that of the birds. The Bishop attempts to be popular with the common people, against the advice of his sister, with little success. His condescension to the Man wearing a Trilby Hat and to the Guardsman meets with little response; his amiability to the chairmen does not extend to practical charity (which is dispensed by his steely sister), nor does the Young Woman's appeal have any effect on him until he realizes her true identity. He can only offer her empty platitudes which have no bearing on the realities of her situation, and when she speaks frankly he tries to retire behind his book.

His ideal of piety, significantly, is the picture of the moral cripples, the Down-and-Out, who have given up the fight of life. He regards them as God's own aristocracy, the "poor in spirit," another reference to the basic principles of true Christianity formulated in the Sermon on the Mount, which O'Casey uses unobtrusively as a yardstick to indicate the falling away of modern society from these standards. It is, he implies, a mistake to equate lack of character and stamina with the true quality of poverty of spirit, an unfortunately ambiguous phrase which really means that genuine humility to which only the great of heart can aspire. To the Bishop, the Down-and-Out are good because they have ceased to fight for their rights, are resigned to the present state of society, submissive to those in authority, and hence are no longer an inconvenience. At last, remorseful for his indifference, the Bishop is converted at the end of the play to a true sense of socialism when he admits that a human soul is not a trivial thing. Like many of O'Casey's characters he leaves the stage a sadder and wiser man, though his change of heart rather weakens his position in the play as a symbol rather than an individual.

The Bishop's Sister is a representative of a harsher religious philosophy. In her rigid piety she has forgotten all sense of human charity and forgiveness. She tries to prevent her brother from following his natural inclination to insure Jannice's safety and is afraid he will come to harm by contact with the common people, showing particular malice, not untinged with sexual envy, against Jannice and her mother, whom she pretends to regard with virtuous disgust.

The deathly propaganda of the two Evangelists is another aspect of contemporary religion. They shuffle in with their depressing reminders of hell-fire religion associated with death and terror, contrasting with O'Casey's worship of life and joy.

The Salvation Army Officer, with his easy method of conversion by facile slogans, is an equally poor representative of Christian faith, and his interest in Jannice is more than a purely professional one. His vanity, too, plays a large part in his enthusiasm for conversions, as he shows in his disappointment at Jannice's preference of the Dreamer.

Finally, the Atheist, the negation of all these, offers a philosophy equally unsatisfactory because it excludes the most necessary things in life—song, dance, joy—all of which form an important part of the author's personal creed.

Throughout the following plays, O'Casey insists that the virtues of youth, joy, and vigor, both physical and mental, must be used to combat the encroaching deadness of modern life, a positive philosophy to resist the negation he feels around him. The dancers, representing natural beauty, are but another form of the natural images which as we have seen, ran through the earlier plays as a contrast to man-made misery, while the Young Woman, who refuses salvation from the various unsatisfactory forms of modern religion, and the Dreamer, whom she follows, are both symbols of the forces of life and beauty which, rather than the false ideals of conventional religion, are O'Casey's gods.

The moral courage of Jannice, who dies dancing, is contrasted with the spiritual deadness of the Down-and-Out, who vainly try to claim her for their own. God, O'Casey would say, can be worshipped far more effectively in the expression of vigor in art and life, than in the empty phrases of those who, while honoring Christianity with their words, have in fact lost all touch with true life, or have become hard and uncharitable, or concentrate on the sentimental or depressing aspects of life. Though attacking conventional religion, as he had done in *The Silver Tassie*, he is not attacking religion as a principle.

In his next play, while certain aspects of religion are condemned in the person of the Purple Priest, he shows approval of the true Christian outlook of the Brown Priest of the people. Always with his Socialist principles in mind, O'Casey condemns that religion which countenances the death of young workers in war, which hypocritically turns away from the class from which its founder sprang, and which supports current social evils, whether the evils of moral corruption or of evil political powers, bolstering a rotten society. His personal religion, which he begins to stress from now on more and more strongly in his plays, is a deep conviction of the holiness of joy, art, love, and youth, together with a truly Christian compassion for human suffering.

His political convictions in the play are a natural development from the ideas of *The Silver Tassie* and earlier plays. He consistently defends the worker against exploitation by the capitalist in peace or war, though admitting that among the moral down-and-out there are many of the working class who are as culpable in their way as the capitalists. His sympathy with the exploited Jannice is characteristic. As Shaw points out in *Mrs. Warren's Profession*, prostitution is merely another form of exploitation, and it is in this light that he presents his heroine.

Thus, his religious philosophy looks back to the previous play in its worship of youthful vigor, the condemnation of hypocritical religion, and concern for the worker. In his next work he stresses both religious and social topics even more explicitly, while preserving the same attitude toward both which he displayed in *The Silver Tassie* and *Within the Gates*.

6

The Rise of the Fascists

In O'Casey's next play, *The Star Turns Red*, his socialist sympathies continue to show themselves as strong as ever in his presentation of the struggle of the two powerful ideologies which loomed over Europe in the 1930's, fascism and communism. In the play, the first is a composite organization, an imaginary force with general coloring from all the Fascist organizations in Germany, England, Ireland, Spain, and Italy. The historical period against which the play is set was full of sinister implications, a time of political as well as economic upheaval, in which events moved inevitably toward a yet more terrible world war. Fascist nations mounted open attacks on their neighbors, the League of Nations disintegrated, Japan took over Manchuria, Italy conquered Abyssinia, Germany prepared to invade Central Europe. Even in democratic countries the Fascist threat began to assert itself; England saw the growth of Oswald Mosely's Black Shirts, Ireland, the Blue Shirts of Eoin O'Duffy. The first triumph of the movement came in the outcome of the Spanish Civil War with the victory of Franco's forces in 1939.

In the play the device of the Circle and the Flash, the symbol of the British Union of Fascists, is referred to by Kian as the symbol of the power which he serves. He walks with a touch of the goose step, which is usually associated with the jackboots of the Nazis, and speaks of "our leader," the English equivalent of

Führer or Duce, while the lashing of Julia is reminiscent of the behavior of O'Duffy's Blue Shirts during the thirties. The Brown Priest warns Red Jim that he will be "sent to a concentration" if he is seized, and the concentration camps of Nazi Germany are brought to mind. Thus the Saffron Shirts, while they have no specific connotation in reference to the contemporary scene, are quite clearly a composite representation of the various forms of fascism growing to power in the contemporary world.

The two forces at work in a divided country reminiscent of Spain during the civil war, then are fascism, supported by the Church, and communism. The workers representing the latter are based on memories of the 1913 Transport and General Workers' Union Strike, when under the leadership of Jim Larkin the workers maintained a prolonged struggle against the Dublin employers before being eventually starved back to work. Larkin, corrupt union officials, staunch Irish workers, all rise from O'Casey's memories of twenty years earlier.

Red Jim is an obvious reference to Jim Larkin, whom O'Casey greatly admired for his pugnacious courage. Physically the two are very similar, with black hair, Herculean physique, expressive face, and hoarse voice. Like his prototype, Red Jim is a master of oratory, as his speech over the dead body of Michael shows, particularly that kind of eloquence which has as its motivating force concrete images of poverty rather than abstract theories. Larkin's figure dominated the Irish scene until his departure for America in much the same way as Red Jim dominates the play. Both men were against drunkenness in their followers, both anxious that benefits and extra money should go to those for whom they were intended rather than into the publican's pocket, and both demanded for their followers more than merely material privileges. Larkin was said to love poetry at least as much as economics, and O'Casey says of him that he would put a flower in a vase on a table in addition to a loaf, while Red Jim protests against the idea that one child shall dwell in the glory of knowledge and another die in the poverty of ignorance.

Both men are physically courageous, Red Jim's bravery being demonstrated in his indifference to the danger of betrayal by Union officials and of capture by the Saffron Shirts. The slogan of his followers, "An Injury to One is the Concern of All," was used by Larkin as the war cry of the sympathetic strike, his most powerful weapon. In his autobiography, O'Casey describes the advent of Larkin in biblical terms to indicate the sacredness of his office as a redeemer of the people, while Red Jim himself uses a biblical style at times: "My comrade was dead, and is alive again; he was lost, and is found!" His trusty henchman Brannigan immediately indicates his Irish origin by his brogue, and is a combination of the qualities of the Christy Mahons and Georgie Middletons, workmates whom O'Casey had the opportunity of studying during his years as a laborer.

The other outstanding members of the Left are less easily recognizable. Though Michael, Jack, and Julia have a touch of Irish in their speech, the last two are merely symbols of Young Love, rather than references to history, and like a similar couple, Monica and Drishogue in a later play, are a trifle dreary.

Not all the labor members are included in the category of heroes. O'Casey had earlier criticized the officials of the trade unions in the person of Jerry Devine in *Juno and the Paycock*, an incidental reference which is much more fully developed in the treacherous, self-seeking bureaucrats of the present play. Sheasker, with his portly figure and gold watch chain, is particularly significant, as these details are in the later plays regarded as the insignia of the capitalist and indicate his disloyalty to the cause of labor. Caheer, thin, mean-looking, and conceited, owns a gold case filled with cigars, a gift from a capitalist friend, Brallain is deceitful, Eglish apathetic, and all are faithlessly disposed to associate with the capitalists, conspiring with the Purple Priest to betray Red Jim.

Sheasker is to act the part of Father Christmas at the Lord Mayor's tea party, sanctimoniously dispensing his condescension to the poor, having first lined his pockets with goods filched from the workers. Ironically above them the slogan of the socialists is stretched: "An Injury to One is the Concern of All," while throughout the scene they reveal themselves in their own treacherous colors.

In his autobiography, O'Casey describes the degeneration of the Labour Party after the departure of Larkin for America, under the timid, respectable leadership of William O'Brien who, he suspects, had given orders to his followers "not to have anything to do with that fellow Casside" (O'Casey's name in the earlier part of the book), when the latter had composed a song, "The Call of the Tribe," to support the labor cause. O'Brien shares with the officials in the play the coldness, vanity, and formality which make him a poor substitute for Larkin, to whose fate he shows much the same indifference as the officials feel for that of Red Jim. Larkin himself was never on good terms with the more conservative of the trade union leaders, whom he would dismiss with a wave of the hand as "penny plain, twopence colored," while they on their part regarded him with alarm and often hostility.

The whole evocation of the troubled times of 1913

is perhaps a piece of wishful thinking, contrasting in its happy outcome with the actual, the bitter ending of the struggle, and with the more recent victory of fascism in Spain in 1939. That is perhaps why in this play the Communists are, after all, toy soldiers who knock down their adversaries with a flick of the wrist, and have little connection with the modern realities of the armed putsch and Red Army liberation. Yet O'Casey does not, as some have suggested, use his political convictions merely as a symbol of the desirable; he is a practical supporter of Soviet communism, and in a passage very similar to the theme of *The Star Turns Red*, he says, "In spite of a swarm of encyclicals wormy with counsels saying sweet is bitter and bitter is sweet; the people are ending the evil. In the uprising of the peoples, the Spirit of God is once more moving over the face of the waters." [1] Among the symptoms of the resurgence of the people, he mentions "the great achievements of the Soviet Union."

Yet the passage above indicates that O'Casey does not merely parrot Socialist creeds. Communism is an atheist philosophy, and O'Casey explicitly states that he sees something divine in the new uprising of the peoples. In *Juno and the Paycock* he had exculpated God from the violence of man, in *The Silver Tassie* he repeated the ideal that God's self-slaying children horrify their creator; the Young Woman dies with the assurance that "[God] will find room for one scarlet blossom," and in the present play the star that turns red is the star of Christmas, and in its change it remains a religious symbol. O'Casey had quarrelled with official republicanism in earlier days in Ireland, while sympathetic to its main tenets, and he diverges from official communism in the same way, though allying himself for better or worse with communism of the specifically Russian kind.

In his intense feeling for the cause, however, and his effort to support it with propaganda, O'Casey had lost much of his sound common sense, his humor, and judgment of human values. Unlike Nora Clitheroe, Julia is expected to be consoled by the glory of the cause for which her lover is sacrificed; the stiff forms which lie around, each with a stiffened clenched fist symbolic of the deathless resolution of the Communists, are there for a quite different purpose from that of the pitiful lean dead hands, indicative of the senseless slaughter of youth, protruding from the rubble in *The Silver Tassie*.

His adroit management of symbols, too, has temporarily deserted him. From one of the windows of the room, factory chimneys are visible; from the other a church may be seen. As the acts progress, the church becomes smaller and the factories larger, symbolizing the weakening of the power of the Church in the lives of the common people, and the corresponding strengthening of communism. The movement of the star from the church to the factory, where it turns red, signifies that true Christianity is no longer to be found in the hypocritical sayings of high churchmen such as the Purple Priest and in the lukewarm principles of *Rerum Novarum*, but in the practical Christianity of socialism. The two windows are labelled by pictures of Lenin and a bishop; the teapot, we are explicitly told, is a symbol of life's necessities, and the crude black table is covered with a tablecloth in the papal colors, symbolic of the domination of the Church over the drab lives of the poor. The aristocratic Purple Priest, at once imperial and funereal in his choice of colors, wears a black girdle as a sign of his opposition to youth and life; the humble brown dress and white girdle of the priest of the people indicate his adherence to the cause of the workers, and of life and youth.

O'Casey's disgust with the part played by the Church in siding with the employer in the class struggle is centered on the figure of the Purple Priest, whose hatred of Red Jim is paralleled by a letter from the Bishop of Sligo to his diocese, read at a service at which Larkin himself was present, warning the workingman of the evils of turning from the priest to the Socialist.

In the play, the Purple Priest is a sinister figure of evil. His association with the Saffron Shirts is immediately shown by his joining in the salute of the Fascists, and represents the alignment of the Church with fascism in many parts of the world during that time, most notably in the alliance of the two powers during the Spanish Civil War. The Church here and from now on in the play is specifically that of Roman Catholicism, which has never been opposed to dictatorship, particularly in Ireland, where Mussolini, Franco, and Salazar have all been held up for admiration by the clergy; and it is notable that during the Spanish Civil War, De Valera had considerable difficulty in withholding the more fanatically religious from thrusting Ireland into the midst of the fighting on the side of the Fascists.

The Purple Priest uses religious principles to discourage the workers from a realization of their true plight. Like the Bishop of *Within the Gates*, who regarded the Down-and-Out as God's own aristocracy, he tells the workers that if they struggle against poverty they will lose the dignity and liveliness that poverty gives the poor—in God's sight, they are clad in gold. Religion, thus, in the hand of the priest of the politicians, becomes a political weapon, and his expression of religious truths becomes merely a parody, a fact emphasized by his droning religious chant based on rhythms of Church ritual. Brutality does not shock him. Like Father Domineer in *Cock-a-Doodle Dandy* and the fanatics in *Behind the Green Curtains*, he approves of driving home the lessons of religion with a stout stick.

O'Casey has shown us before that the gentle Christian religion is often associated with the most appalling violence, here specifically with the flogging of Julia and the murder of Michael. In his narrow suspicion of sex, too, the Purple Priest is associated particularly with the outlook of the Catholic Church in Ireland, which O'Casey was to single out more particularly for satire in three later plays. In all, the Purple Priest is the symbol of a religion antipathetic to joy, suspicious of freedom, and indifferent to the claims of common humanity.

Another aspect of religion is suggested by the "Catholic flag-wagger," Joybell, a close relation of John Jo Mulligan in *Bedtime Story*. Both young men are diverted from their pious preoccupations to more natural interests by the efforts respectively of Julia and Angela. Joybell has the jollity which goes with thoughtless and unquestioning acceptance of Church doctrine and is blithely ignorant of human problems, from which he is shielded by his impregnable cheeriness and native piety. As in the case of Rankin in *The Bishop's Bonfire*, the suppression of his instincts has the effect of causing him to be particularly brutal, partly from panic, when tempted to indulge them. He is representative of a certain section of the Catholic laity—enthusiastic, jolly, militant, ignorant of the true nature of the problems they try to answer with ready-made dogmatic formulas.

Yet, as in the early plays, O'Casey, while attacking conventional religion, does not attack religion in principle. He rather tries to show that practical Christianity is to be found now in socialism rather than in the Church, which is now merely the bulwark of a capital-

ist society and has abandoned the workers. The Brown
Priest's shift of loyalty to Red Jim is as significant as
the changing position of the star from the church
steeple to the factory chimneys. As his convictions
grow, he abandons his support of the lukewarm
Rerum Novarum, with its inadequate social principles,
warns Red Jim of his danger, and, though still with
the Purple Priest when the latter comes to claim Michael's body, is at last seen climbing over the barri-
cades to join the Socialists at the height of the battle.
It is he who utters the lines which form the core of
the play.

> I serve my Master here.
> In the loud clamour made by war-mad men
> The voice of God may still be heard;
> And, in a storm of curses, God can bless.
> The star turned red is still the star
> Of him who came as man's pure prince of peace;
> And so I serve him here.

The Purple Priest departs, leaving behind him the
victorious Red Jim and the Brown Priest as comrades.
The character of the latter is brought to mind by some
words of W. P. Ryan.

> Some younger priests see the irony and humiliation of
> the . . . un-Christian spectacle of Catholic ecclesiastics
> as impassioned defenders of worldly property, honour-
> ing the rich or well-to-do in this world and bidding the
> poor be content with the prospect of heaven in the
> next; forgetting or ignoring the fact that the Catholic
> ideal is collectivist, not individualistic as the term is
> usually understood.[2]

Thus on both sides the opposing parties are divided
from within, the Brown Priest breaking away from the
Purple Priest as the trade union officials break away
from Red Jim. Although at first the play would appear

to be exclusively Communist in sympathy, closer examination shows that a principal theme is that of true religion, and the principles of applied Christianity in socialism, to which O'Casey unfailingly adheres in his plays. In the next work, the fight against the enemies of socialism continues, this time with the background of the Second World War, in which the Allies stood with Communist Russia against the common Fascist enemy.

7

The Second World War

The inevitable development of world affairs in 1939 again presented O'Casey with the spectacle of an international war, and, as in 1928, he attempted in 1946 to force what he had seen into dramatic mold, this time with considerably less success. He invites comparison of the present work, *Oak Leaves and Lavender*, with his last great war play by the subtitle, *A World on Wallpaper*, a reference to Yeats's criticism of *The Silver Tassie*, in which he commented that the Great War obtruded itself too much in the play, which should use current events merely as "wallpaper in front of which the characters must pose and speak." [1] Yeats's comment, as Shaw remarked to O'Casey, was undiscerning.

The protagonist of *The Silver Tassie* is not Harry Heegan or his friends; it is the war itself, and it had never been O'Casey's intention to use it as mere period color or incidental background. He deliberately brought it out of the wallpaper background to the front of the stage. In connection with the present play, however, Yeats's criticism would have been more justified, for it is a strange mixture of undigested opinions and ideas, none of which have been burned up by dramatic action, and its failure is of the same kind and attributable to the same causes as that of *The Star Turns Red*—it is a piece of propaganda masquerading as drama, and would have been happier in the form of a political tract.

It is among the most topical of O'Casey's plays, however, and therefore merits detailed discussion in the consideration of his use of social and political material. He brings to mind many reminiscences of the time when the people at home in England were suffering the consequences of the war abroad, sometimes tragically in air raids, sometimes comically in their struggle with the inevitable red tape which accompanies the reorganization of a country's life. The play is punctuated with references which vividly recall the early days of the Second World War. It would appear, however, that though the period is specifically dated as taking place during the Battle of Britain, which places it between July and October, 1940, O'Casey has included several events which took place outside those dates. Feelim has to supervise the distribution of gas masks, although this had already been done during the Munich crisis; and we are shown the arrival of American arms, which in fact only came when Roosevelt's lend-lease arrangement was settled, long after the Battle of Britain. Thus a certain telescoping of events has taken place.

The historical background of the time is well known and needs little comment. The authoritative account is to be found in Winston Churchill's *The Second World War*. Germany's demand for *lebensraum*, or living space, mentioned by Deeda Tutting, had been granted on several occasions, when the aggressive policy of Hitler spread German rule into Austria, the Sudetenland, and Czechoslovakia with no firm protest from the Allies, until it was realized that German expansion was in fact an attempt at world domination. During this period, Germany was in the grip of the Nazi (National Socialist) Party, which Deeda feels is in many respects superior to Soviet, British, or French systems of government, apart from its racial animosity. The latter was the doctrine of the

superiority of the German "race" and consequent in-
feriority of all others, particularly the Jewish, which,
international and peaceful, was directly opposed to
this nationalistic and belligerent philosophy. The arm
of the party was the notorious Gestapo (an abbrevia-
tion of *Geheime Staatspolizen*), the secret state po-
lice-force in Germany from 1933 to 1945, an offshoot
of the *Schutzstaffel* or S.S., Hitler's personal body-
guard. In effect the Gestapo was the counterpart of
the Russian O.G.P.U. attacked by Deeda; each was an
arm of a totalitarian state, neither subject to legal or
moral restrictions.

The final aggressive move of Hitler, his defiant invasion of Poland, plunged the world into a war which at
first seemed to be a mortal disaster to the unprepared
allies. In June, 1940, the defenses of France finally
gave way and the frantic evacuation of Dunkirk became one of the memorable events of the war. Feelim
is well aware of the dangers to which England is now
exposed and exhorts those around him to realize that
with the retreat of the remnants of the army from
Dunkirk they are left to face the Germans "pilin' into
the barges all along the coasts less than twenty miles
away from us." The threat of invasion was an ever-pre-
sent one during the early stages of the war, an almost
inconceivable danger to an island which had not suffered an invasion since 1066, but real nevertheless.
Many of the "better people" made determined efforts
to escape to America, and the terrified Constant, ironically named, provides us with an example of the
current fears. Churchill's famous uncompromising
speeches to the British people during the early months
of the war had also left their mark on Feelim, who
faithfully echoes his incitement to fight in the field
and in the streets if necessary, rather than submit to
the invaders.

After the collapse of France in 1940, Britain stood

alone against the Axis powers, and the struggle known as the Battle of Britain took place. This struggle was centered upon air power. All the resources of the *Luftwaffe* were directed against the Royal Air Force, and the courage shown by the latter called forth Churchill's famous tribute, "Never in the field of human conflict was so much owed by so many to so few." The average life of an airman, at this time, Edgar remarks, was no more than eight weeks. In September the final major fight took place, and as a result Hitler decided to postpone his plan for the invasion of Britain (operation Sea Lion), owing to the efforts of the "few," among whom young Drishogue and Edgar are found. The civilians pay them tribute as they go to take their part in the Battle of Britain: "Young, lusty lads in Air Force blue, / Go forth wearing red rose and rue; / Our life, our dreams, depend on you, / Sons of England!" The red rose is a patriotic symbol and also an emblem of vigor, joy, and sacrifice, as will be shown in the discussion of *Red Roses for Me*; rue is the symbol of grief for those who will not return.

The patriotic enthusiasm of the crowd is mingled with anti-Irish feeling. During the Second World War, De Valera remained prudently neutral and, late in 1939, Churchill, lamenting the loss of the West Coast ports, which had been returned to Ireland against his advice, voiced the suspicion and anxiety which characterized the average Englishman's attitude toward Ireland at this time. He spoke of the possible succoring of U-boats by Irish malevolents in the West of Ireland inlets, for, he said, if they throw bombs in London why should they not supply fuel to U-boats?

An implacable minority still resentful of the partition of Ireland continued spasmodic aggressive acts against England, and the English, debarred from the use of such ports as Berehaven, felt justifiably anxious at the possibility of an enemy at their back door. Dame Hatherleigh bursts out, "You damned Irish! Why didn't your selfish people come over to help us?" —a sentiment later echoed by Pobjoy, the Old Woman, Felicity, and Joy. Feelim replies to their criticisms of the valor of the Irish by a history of Irish participation in English wars since the Conquest. He perhaps represents the "three-quarters of the people of Southern Ireland" mentioned by Churchill who supported the English in the struggle—certainly O'Casey seems to feel that old differences should be forgotten in the crisis. He represents Feelim as an admirable character, respected by his neighbors, a true Irishman, as he shows from his knowledge of the old myths of the Tuatha de Danaan and Tara, the old seat of the Irish High Kings; yet he spends time and energy in urging the people to greater efforts, squabbles with the foreman who supports De Valera's neutrality, and finally gives his son to the cause. The alliance of Celt and Anglo-Saxon in the common fight against fascism is further underlined by the emphasis on Monica's Celtic origin—all the old feuds are to be forgotten in the greater cause against the common enemy.

Meanwhile, the Battle of Britain was giving place to the Battle of London, an intensive attack on the capital, lasting between August, 1940 and May, 1941. From November, 1940, onward the enemy attempted the systematic disorganization and destruction of key factories and centers of war production. All important industrial centers were visited at this time, and Joy remarks that "Duxton got it hot." There is in fact no record of attacks on any town of this name, but in the light of O'Casey's own experiences, described in the last volume of his autobiography, *Sunset and Evening*

Star, it would seem that the real reference was to the devastating attacks on Plymouth. The civilians and the members of the forces were urged to wear identity disks made of metal or some indestructable material, in order to make identification easier in case of death. It was for these that the searchers looked among the wreckage of Drishogue's plane.

It is clear that the background of the play is based on the history of the southwest of England during the early part of the war, and the blitzed town referred to is probably Plymouth, an inference strengthened by Monica's claim to be a "Cornish lass," and the southern dialect of the characters.

Aerodromes were among the favorite targets of the *Luftwaffe,* since it was their aim to disable the British planes before they had a chance to leave the ground. The first aerodrome to be attacked was at Catterick in May, 1940, another detail that helps to date the play. The aerodrome where Edgar and Drishogue were killed must have been bombed after this date.

Among the most widely used weapons of the attackers was the incendiary bomb, which caused the fires of London seen by the dancers and the "blazin' buildin's" seen by Mrs. Watchit. Delayed-action bombs were also in use, which, being fitted with a time mechanism, failed to explode when they fell and immobilized important railway junctions and long stretches of track, blocked main roads, and made it necessary to evacuate many citizens from their homes. It would seem that it was one of these delayed-action bombs that the drunken Abe found on the window sill. The government was well aware of the menace of these weapons and by the end of October, 1940, some seven hundred people were engaged in the dangerous work of the Royal Engineers Bomb Disposal Section, though even then the number of such bombs to be dealt with remained at about three thousand and, as Mark points out, the government emphatically warned people against touching unfamiliar objects. The psychological attack coming over the radio was perhaps more insidious. It urged the British people to throw out their government and capitulate. The signal "Germany Calling," which is heard at appropriate moments as the cloth of the wireless panel lights up to show the Nazi symbol of the swastika, was particularly associated with the work of a renegade Englishman, William Joyce, popularly known as "Lord Haw-Haw" on account of his elegant accent. Other methods of attack, apart from those thus used on the home front, were the wide use of submarines or U-boats, particularly those in the Atlantic, a fact Joy mentions in a conversation with Jennie. Shipping in this area suffered heavily by their activities, and many vessels were torpedoed in the manner described by Feelim from the firsthand information of his friend.

The methods of attack mentioned in the play were counteracted by the government in various ways. A.R.P. (Air Raid Precautions), or Civil Defence, as it came to be called, was an immense and complicated organization. It had begun as far back as 1923, when the Committee of Imperial Defence decided to appoint an Air Raid Precautions Committee under the chairmanship of the Permanent Undersecretary of State for the Home Department. In 1935 an Air Raid Precautions Department was set up at the Home Office. The organization grew rapidly in the years immediately before the war, and among its many responsibilities were anti-gas measures, casualty and mortuary services, camouflage, fire service, rescue and demolition services, warden's service, and many others.

The warden's service is of particular interest here,

since Feelim was a head warden. The warden was, ideally, a responsible member of the public, chosen to be the leader and adviser of his neighbors in a small area or group of streets where he was known and respected. This gives us some idea of the strength and responsibility of Feelim's character. By July, 1939, the original plan for a warden's post for each sector of five hundred inhabitants was dropped, and under the new scheme a number of them were worked from one post. Sectors were in the charge of senior wardens, a group of these forming a post, which would be the responsibility of any one of the senior wardens. Posts in turn were formed into groups, each serving a population of six to ten thousand and in the charge of a head warden. Thus Feelim was responsible for the safety of several thousand people, and by implication a respected and responsible man.

The nature of the use to which the manor is put is manifold. As Feelim's headquarters it is an Air Raid Warden's Post. It is also used as a rest center for bombed-out victims of the raids (by May, 1940, the homeless in rest centers were estimated at over seventy thousand). Later it evolves into a factory.

Feelim has all the equipment for his job. In 1938, at the time of the Munich crisis, wardens were issued gas masks and steel helmets such as he puts on at the end of the play. His duties are bewildering and onerous, including, among others the "stirrup-pump class," to teach the use of this light, cheap hand pump, fitted with a support for the foot from which it took its name, specially made to control fires caused by incendiary bombs. They were issued to local authorities at the outbreak of the war and, in April, 1940, the loan of pumps to fire authorities for the training of the public was begun.

With his varied duties, Feelim is almost overwhelmed in a mesh of blackout restrictions and red tape. His main troubles as the play opens derive from the former—"Th' house'll be an hospital before this blackout's finished," he cries in despair, as another victim is injured in the effort to black out the windows of the old manor.

In November, 1938, the Committee of Imperial Defense gave final approval to the blackout, a term used for a number of years to signify the severest lighting restrictions practicable in time of war. Early in February all local authorities were told of the drastic measures which would impose general darkening as a permanent condition from the outbreak of war. The Civil Defense Bill of March, 1939, made it finally clear that the blackout was absolutely compulsory, and the early months of the war found many others besides Monica and Feelim struggling with yards of thick black cloth. Since the restrictions were brought into force on Friday, September 1, 1939, Monica and Feelim are late with their preparations if the Battle of Britain is to be accepted literally as the date of the play—here again we have evidence of telescoping. One of the well-known cries of the war became "Put that light out," the stentorian call of the patrolling policeman; and Feelim begins to feel that there is a constable behind every bush. Dillery's vigilance is shown later in the play when with Sillery he comes to investigate the lights shown by Monica, Drishogue, and Feelim.

Windows received further attention as they were crisscrossed by strips of adhesive paper or, alternately, treated with window security paint, both intended to prevent splintering under pressure from the blast of a bomb. Sandbags were liberally used to absorb the blast of bombs, and most large buildings were provided with them. Mark prefers adhesive paper, Michael, the paint, while Dame Hatherleigh feels sand-bags would be more effective.

Another memorable feature of the war was the warn-ing siren which indicated the approach of raiders. In 1938 separate warning districts were defined in detail, and numbered more than a hundred. The authorities distributed the warnings by telephone in simple spo-ken messages, yellow being the code for "preliminary caution," red for "action warning," green for "raiders passed," white for "cancel caution." Later a purple message was introduced as a warning to all districts not expected to be the object of the attack. This explains the purple light that glows over the globe on the clock and is pointed out by Dame Hatherleigh as the warning of a raid. The manor itself is not an objective, but would be in the track of bombers mak-ing for the nearby aerodrome. The term alert came to be used for any type of air raid, hence the use of the term by Joy at the beginning of Act II.

Among other measures of safety for the public was the distribution of the Anderson shelter, a practical household device limited to large towns in the most vulnerable areas. Those entitled to free issue were householders compulsorily in the National Health In-surance Scheme (the majority of manual workers) and those with an income of not more than £250 a year. The complaints of the people in the play, how-ever, may have had some foundation in view of the fact that when war broke out, the needs of the main danger zones had not been met, since production of the shelters had achieved only two-thirds of the esti-mated aim, and of those which had been installed, some had been fitted so badly as to be almost worthless.

More active defense was supplied by the Home Guard, whose efforts at soldiering are so contemp-

tuously regarded by Feelim. The organization was
formed on May 14, 1939, as the Local Defence Volunteers, a supplement to the regular army for the defense
of the island, and soon came to number more than
one million. They were, at least in theory, armed, and
subject when on duty to military discipline, though
the "arms," as seen in the play, were at first no more
than agricultural implements. Mark and Michael
wield, with considerable danger to their friends, pikes
with shafts of fourteen feet and blades of two feet,
causing Feelim much concern. This would indicate a
date of early 1940, when rifles were scarce.

Yet these men, working amateurishly but enthusiastically, were worthy of recognition, and on September
3, 1940, George VI broadcast his intention to recog-
nize deeds of gallantry by creating a new mark of
honor for men and women in all walks of civilian life
—the George Cross (won by Farmer Penrhyn), and
the George Medal for wider distribution (won by
Sillery).

In addition to the defensive effort against raids and
attacks, another side of the war effort took place in
England. Eligible women not conscripted into one of
the armed forces (such as the Women's Auxiliary Air
Force, and the Auxiliary Territorial Service, representatives of which make a silent appearance in the play)
were obliged to work either in munitions or on the
land, and the types of workers became very mixed, the
great majority being represented by the coarse, easy-
living pair of land girls in the play. The different levels
of education available at the time are indicated by the
fact that Jennie has had the advantage of a secondary
or grammar school education, while Joy has had to be
satisfied with an ordinary council school upbringing,
that is to say she comes from an elementary school
run by local authorities.

The cultivation of home produce led to another famous wartime slogan, "Dig for Victory," to which Feelim imagines the Dame is referring when she speaks of her archeological dreams. Everyone was expected to do his bit toward the war effort—as Feelim says, everyone strong enough to bend a blade of grass had to get going. The V for victory sign was yet another topical reference; the two upraised fingers of Churchill, the Morse signal over the radio, the placards all over the country were meant to raise the morale of the people and remind them, as Dame Hatherleigh wishes to do with her big, white V sign, that victory is sure. The point is reechoed when Dillery makes the V sign as he rushes in with news of the arrival of American arms.

Yet much of the war effort was concerned with mundane and unromantic subjects; the meticulous saving of fuel, which causes Feelim and Mrs. Watchit so much trouble, was a source of endless bewilderment to most householders during the period. They flounder in a tangle of forms and official papers, a fair sample of which is Feelim's account of the order concerning rhubarb.

One more point of contemporary interest remains: the arms which arrive so opportunely from America. As already indicated, this in fact took place later than the date of the play, as the Lend-Lease Bill was signed in 1941. The rejoicings over the arrival, however, provide an effective contrast to the news of Dame Hatherleigh's loss. O'Casey has telescoped history in order to employ his favorite technique of playing off the tragic against a contrast.

Such, then, is the historical setting of the play. The moral is pointed by the ghostly figures of the Prelude. They appear drifting around a great manorial house of a long-past century. The house is England, haunted by the past in all its greatness and corruption, threatened by the danger of the Second World War. The idea of a symbolic house recurs in *Purple Dust,* when the house which is finally submerged represents the power of capitalism.

At the opening of the present play, we see that the house had potentialities of great mechanical resources which are realized more and more fully as the play progresses, just as England over a period was converted from a land of gracious living for the few to a nation whose every effort was bent to the production of armaments for war. Feelim indicates the same theme when, at the end of the play, he abandons the familiar romantic symbol of past England (Hearts of Oak) for the modern version (Hearts of Steel).

The common purpose of the English people during these years did more to break down class barriers than any Socialist propaganda. During the period in which the play takes place, there was no aspect of English life unaffected by the frantic scramble to overtake German armament manufacture, which had gradually exceeded those of the victors of the First World War during the 1930's. In the Prelude, only the suggestions of mechanization are seen. In the first act, the tendency is stressed, since the paneling seems a little more stylized away from its normal lines and curving, while by Act III the big room has changed with the changing world outside it. The house which is England is converted by the machinery which is now plainly seen. Dame Hatherleigh with obvious significance says, "The House must change; but it must not die," while the ordeal of England is pointed by the crowd: "The house is trembling and the windows shake!"

This, then, is the house in modern times, yet it is framed by the past. The vague forms of the eighteenth-century dancers, Sir Nigel, who died at Blenheim, and his bride, drift through the rooms at the beginning of the play, and throughout the characters fighting the war of 1940 are conscious of the scent of lavender and the rustle of skirts reminding them of dead generations. To Edgar's comment that the past can never have any influence on us, Drishogue replies, "the past has woven us into what we are." The subtle influence of the dead on their posterity, symbolized by the scent of lavender which drifts through the rooms, seems to have been a principal idea in O'Casey's mind.

The influence is not altogether bad. In *Purple Dust*, an earlier play to be considered later, O'Casey's contempt for the past as a symbol of capitalist domination is clearly underlined. Here the past has good things to offer, since it is the past of Goldsmith, Berkeley, Boyle, Addison, Hone, Swift, and Sheridan. These are the gifts of the past, to be salvaged from the general wreckage of society. The utter contempt O'Casey had for the past in *Purple Dust* may be explained by the fact that there the past was medieval, and O'Casey is a firm opponent of medievalism, as will be shown later; here he is dealing with the rationalist eighteenth century. The same theme of the passing of the power from the hands of the old nobility is still sounded, however, by the Young Son of Time, who comments, to the disquiet of the aristocratic dancers, that "Time has put them [torches] into the itching hand of the people."

In the same way, the present characters who die leave their impression on the living who follow them. Drishogue dies at the end of the play, but he leaves in Monica's unborn child a living spark from himself. The continuity of life, physically and spiritually, is emphasized. Dame Hatherleigh at the end of the play fades into the company of the ghostly dancers with her memories (represented by a silver cap); all signs of life (dark-green suit, crimson-flecked orange scarf) are swallowed up by her long sable cloak, yet "Our end makes but a beginning for others," she says, and as she slips out of the world Monica's child is about to be born into it. Leaves are continually springing from the oak tree, which gives promise that the "Hearts of Oak" will pass on their valor to their posterity. The new, socialist society of the future will not deprive life of color, as Dame Hatherleigh assures the Third Lady Dancer, and from the exclamation of her partner O'Casey takes the title of the play. "The lavender will bloom again, and oak leaves laugh at the wind in the storm"—the gracious elegance of the past and the sturdy courage of the present will survive into the future. The mechanization of the future holds no terrors; the great belts and wheels of the machinery which fills the old house are colored with associations of life, spring, and growth, for the unpromising, angular shapes of the machines are in fact the workers' assurance of a better life for the common people.

All this would have formed a worthwhile theme if O'Casey had made full use of it. As in *The Star Turns Red*, however, certain propagandist ideas seem to obtrude themselves whether he will or not. One is Russian communism, the other a by now rather stale repetition of the "young, free love" theme first seen in *Within the Gates*.

The latter group of ideas, based on a worship of youth, joy, and vigor, finds expression in the land-girl Jennie, who has many of the signs which O'Casey regards as symbolic of vitality, an attractive figure and an emblematic touch of green, the color also associated with the past valor of Drishogue and in a darker shade with the ebbing life of the Dame, as shown by the green slip over his coffin and the dark green of her costume. Jennie is the mouthpiece of O'Casey's philosophy, which she underlines with the occasional bawdy song, and she ends as a martyr to it by dying in the flames with Drishogue. The other young people in various degrees echo the same theme, sometimes with embarrassingly cheap melodrama, as when Monica, in opposition to her mean old father, invites Drishogue to "Take me in your arms to my room again, an' show him I am lost for ever!" Dame Hatherleigh is also associated with the life and vigor theme, yet she too is a disappointment. She reminds us vaguely of Lady Gregory; both lost a son by violent death in war, both have an almost obsessive preoccupation: Lady Gregory with the recovery of the Lane pictures, which went to the British government after the death of her nephew, Sir Hugh Lane, on the "Lusitania"; Dame Hatherleigh with the Ten Tribes of Israel. Yet she is an unsatisfactory character and fades into the company of the dancers after the death of her son.

The second theme is that of communism. Drishogue seems to have the task of linking this theme to the previous one in his dual capacity of Communist and Young Lover, though he is consistently tedious whichever way he is taken. He defends his politics in the scene with Deeda Tutting, taken almost word for word from the incident in *Sunset and Evening Star* where Creda Stern comes to convert O'Casey to anti-communism by recounting the fate of her husband at the hands of the O.G.P.U., but both the playwright and his character are obstinately deaf to the very reasonable objections against the abduction of the lady's husband—"And the more you shout, lady, the less I hear" is O'Casey's attitude. The vocabulary and style of Drishogue's utterances are reminiscent of the highly colored oratory of Connolly and Larkin in O'Casey's youth, from whom he derived his Socialist principles, and which have in truth little relevance to the modern realities of the totalitarian state. A contemporary reference is made to Dr. Hewlett Johnson, the "Red Dean" of Canterbury, whose book *The Socialist Sixth of the World* had evidently been read by Feelim, and also to the Spanish Civil War, in which Drishogue, unlike his forerunner, O'Killigain in *Purple Dust*, had been too young to take part.

The average Englishman of 1940 did not perhaps feel so unqualified an enthusiasm for Russia as O'Casey's young hero. The clear-cut opposition of the totalitarian ideologies was not fully appreciated even in the Kremlin itself, for Stalin had actually made agreements with Hitler at the beginning of the war and had no intention of entering the war against him until Hitler's ill-judged attack on the Red Army brought about the uneasy alliance of the U. S. S. R. and the Western democracies. Deeda in fact mentions the possibility of a collaboration between Russia and Germany, but this is taken as an empty absurdity.

Since *The Silver Tassie* O'Casey's views on peace and war have undergone a change. In the play he saw realistically the horrors of war, since the First World War was brought about by the capitalists for their own interests and was merely another aspect of the exploitation of the common man. Now, however, his personal convictions are involved; the war of Red Jim against fascism was condoned in *The Star Turns Red*, and here too the struggle of the Allies in line with Russia against the Axis powers assumes the aspect of the sacred class war, which alone is permissible. Drishogue makes it clear that he is fighting the Fascists who had created havoc in Spain, rather than the enemies of England as such—the fight is merely an extension of the Spanish Civil War. The unnatural horrors of death in battle become a romantic alternative to the miseries of old age; in the present play, the night-mare of war is relegated to the dreams of a hysterical old woman.

Pacifists are now objects of scorn. Pobjoy, the con-scientious objector, is a miserable creature compared with the romantic Drishogue. He presents a curious spectacle, moving shamefacedly through the play like the reproachful ghost of an abandoned ideal. Pacifism is again guyed in the form of old Abraham who, with all his private cruelty, is yet a pacifist in principle and boasts of never having taken a life.

Oak Leaves and Lavender concludes a group of four plays on themes of world events of which only two, *The Silver Tassie* and *Within the Gates,* are dramati-cally successful. Consideration of these four works as a group is useful since it enables us to understand cer-tain principles of O'Casey's work. One of his main objects of satire is conventional religion, which has abandoned true Christian principles. As a positive replacement, O'Casey offers his own highly personal creed of the virtues and saving power of youth, love, and art, and the sacredness of human life. This, how-ever, gives way when he endorses the bloody war against fascism, abandons his pacifist principles, and uneasily upholds the Socialist doctrine according to which it is a glorious duty of the young to die for the cause. The probability that he is not at heart in sym-pathy with the sentiments of his death-or-glory heroes, Red Jim and Drishogue, may account for the dramatic failure of the last two plays of the group.

8

Back to Ireland — A Comic Vision

The date fixed for the action of *Purple Dust* is "the
present day," which places it in 1940 at the beginning
of the Second World War. Of recent times, according
to Edmund J. Murray, "there is an ever-increasing
flow of English gentlemen of means into the Republic
—men who are leaving the burning ship of the English state and crossing over to John Bull's former island, buying up estate after estate and settling down
to the traditionally Irish leisurely way of life." [1] The
differences of the two "races," naturally emphasized
by their close proximity and aggravated by the antagonism which as we have seen prevailed between them
during the war provided O'Casey with plenty of material for a study of English-Irish relationships.

Churchill's official expression of suspicion reflected
the general feeling and resentment of the English
people as a whole, and when O'Casey brought out his
anti-English satire it seemed like a nasty stab in the
back of a great nation struggling for freedom against a
common enemy. But he speaks of the ostrich-like policy of Ireland: "She had shut out all mention and
meddle with the U. S. S. R., shut out Joyce, O'Casey,
and allowed Shaw only to look over the garden wall;
and now she set about shutting out the war." [2]

Later he gibes at the meanness of Irish satisfaction
at English difficulties during and after the war; some
Irish, he says, sent up a titter that England would
soon be as the old Bards had foretold—trudging

through the frost without a shoe on her foot, a prophecy recalled with satisfaction by the Second Workman in the play.

Yet however much his comments elsewhere may
indicate criticism of the attitude of modern Ireland,
his position in the present play is one of approbation
for the Irish and scathing contempt for the English
blunderers who intrude upon them. The unpopularity
of the play and Agate's comment that it was a worthless work and an attack on England when England
was helpless and unable to reply are not surprising.
But on closer examination, it is questionable whether
Agate and his fellow patriots were right. Certainly the
Irish-English conflict does enter into it, but it is by no
means the central point of the play. A too easy association with Shaw's *John Bull's Other Island* can easily obscure the issue, as in Jules Koslow's account of
the play: "G. B. Shaw had been intrigued with the
same idea." [3] A careful consideration of the two plays
side by side makes it clear that it was not the same
idea at all. Shaw's play is a clever account of the basic
differences between the two "races"; Broadbent is ro-
bust, energetic, eager, and credulous, sometimes
shrewd and roguish, portenously solemn at times,
sometimes jolly and irresible, mostly likeable, and on
the whole enormously absurd—in other words, the
Irishman's view of the typical Englishman.

Contrasted with Broadbent, the "English" characters in *Purple Dust* are strange characters. They are no
more recognizably English than the Irish in the play
are truly Irish. At one point only, in his exaggerated
claims for the integrity of England, does Poges approach the characteristic absurd pomposity of Broad-
bent, when he claims that "Justice is England's old
nurse, Righteousness and Peace sit together in her
common-room, and the porter at her gate is Truth."

Thus, except in such occasional echoes of Broad-bent, Poges and Stoke are not primarily Englishmen. Regarded in the light of the previous plays, however, their true nature becomes clear. They are not so much Englishmen as capitalists. Poges is inclined to be stout, with a heavy physique and a too prominent belly—his face is broad and ruddy, and there are bags of flesh under his eyes. Under his smock, he wears morning clothes and a top hat; with his companions he comes out of the city; he and Stoke are business-men, rolling in money, and he is according to himself a "money'd man," with power over others, while according to the Second Workman he is a "smoky brag-ger who thinks th' world spins round on th' rim of a coin." His conscientious love of the country is incon-sequential beside his anxiety to get in contact with his agent in London to secure his business interests, and his conversation on the telephone indicates that he is one of the men "lookin' after business"—mentioned by the Second Soldier in *The Silver Tassie*—who make money out of war. On realizing that others have got there before him in the race for profits out of the war, Poges exclaims virtuously against those who try to make money out of splintered bodies. He protests against the striking workers and has doubled Stoke's income for him by wise investment; he reads the *Financial Universe* and staunchly upholds imperialism. Hence we have the old conflict under a new guise—the capitalist-worker struggle, which has entered into each of the last four plays.

Stoke represents another aspect of the governing classes; if Poges is the self-made capitalist, his com-panion is the university man. Stoke is an intellectual, proud of his ill-digested erudition and aristocratic de-scent. The two men come into conflict briefly as the latter tries to air his learning and is met with contempt by the self-made Poges. "Almost weeping" during the argument, he is perhaps reminiscent of the "eager and delicately mannered" Beverley Nichols, the "Princess Charming of English literature," whom O'Casey met and disliked on his arrival in London. He, like Stoke, was a product of Oxford, and O'Casey immediately summed him up as "a toff." Nichols' interest in "getting back to nature" and his dislike of the big city was increased when in the thirties he acquired a country cottage and wrote sentimentally of it in his book A *Village in a Valley*, of which Basil's philosophy of universals and primroses is reminiscent.

There are certain things which O'Casey regards as symbols of hated capitalist domination. The past, especially the medieval past, which implies for him oppression of the people by the Church, the exclusion of the working classes from the universities, and the false romanticism of the concept of "Merry England," always arouse his anger. Here, with his capitalists worshipping at the shrine of the good old days, he has plenty of scope for satire. The ancient subservience of Christian nations to the Church during that period seems now only to survive in Ireland, as he makes clear in the later plays, where he deals with the realities of the Irish situation.

Throughout his autobiography, O'Casey clearly associates the Middle Ages with the bad old days of capitalist and clerical domination. In *Rose and Crown*, he explains his feeling against the big houses of the past and the futility of trying to save them and what they symbolize: "Now a cry has gone forth to save the broken turrets of the Big Houses . . . that are dropping their stones . . . and give back a lacquered life to the gentry who live in them. Let them become pensioners of the State; tax the workers so that the gentry may be there for the workers to go and see how they live; and come away civilized." [4]

This is the spirit of *Purple Dust,* and beside it the incidental Irish-English conflict takes second place. The two capitalists worship the past in which the capitalist ruled supreme, with the help of the Church, at the expense of the people; yet, as O'Casey points out in his autobiography, this was the "base of misery [which] kept up this lacquered superstructure of charm and graciousness."

The feeling is unquestionably the dominant one of the play. In the opening scene, O'Killigain and the First Workman outline their attitude to the fools who worship the past and admire ruinous houses for the sake of "some titled tomfool" who may have resided there. The house itself is symbolic—its rottenness is the rottenness of capitalist society, as is made clear by Poges's account of the rich luxurious life of its past aristocratic inhabitants who were, says the First Workman, "all halo'd with scents to bring them round from th' smell o' th' poor an' dingier world at work or play." By the sly encouragement of the First Workman, Poges is led on to all sorts of absurdities in conjuring up the dead days of the past, but O'Killigain voices O'Casey's views when he says "I let the dead bury their dead." The big house of Stoke and Poges is doomed to destruction as surely as Shaw's equally symbolic Heartbreak House. In both play and autobiography, O'Casey foretells the fall of the big houses: "The revolt against the Big Houses has come even into the hearts and minds of the younger members of the grandee families . . . the house and the things in the house themselves had become objects of a life that had passed away for ever." He pictures the house invaded by the triumphant workers, just as in the play it is inundated by the purifying flood of the rising tide of socialism: "The Communes are comin', and the Big Houses are in the way of their march. The Big Houses must go with the times. The People are debouching from the public roads into private property."

The theme in *Purple Dust* is clearly summarized here. In the play the development of the same theme includes an explanation of the title of the play: "You have had your day, like every dog. Your Tudors have had their day, and they are gone; and th' little heap o' purple dust they left behind them will vanish away in th' flow of the river." Earlier the Second Workman voices his regret that the great deeds of the past are now but "a little cloud o' purple dust blown before the wind." The dust represents the past, principally the unworthy past of capitalist England, but also the glorious past of Ireland.

Against this background of two foolish representatives of capitalist society trying in vain to bolster up the symbolic house which is falling apart, we see as before the heroic workers upholding the cause of the common man while engaging in the profitable occupation of spoiling the Egyptians. O'Killigain, the handsome, sensitive young hero, wears a muffler, the insignia of the worker, and has read widely; he has fought, like Jack and Drishogue, against the Fascists; he defends youth, life, and joy against the attacks of the clergy, and eventually carries off Poges's sweetheart.

The Second Workman is a rather more complex character, combining in himself the roles of Irishman, worker, comic, and second "junior lead." As a worker he stands with O'Killigain against the capitalists and carries off the second most attractive girl, while as Irishman he expounds to the bewildered Poges his mystic vision of the great spirits of Ireland. Here there is an unmistakeable reference to O'Casey's similar teasing of Baldwin in *Rose and Crown,* where the traditional conception of the clever Irishman and the stupid Englishman is brought into the play. A land of scintillating illogicality is a favorite conception of Ireland, especially by Irishmen, and Baldwin, like Poges, flounders helplessly in the "Seltic Twilight." Like Baldwin, Poges attempts to copy the Irish idiom in his speech with ludicrous results, and both adopt an attitude of patronizing condescension, as to an inferior race: "A wonderful people, if only agitators would leave them alone," Baldwin says. "Bit backward, perhaps, like all primitive peoples . . . but delightful people all the same," Poges says. Both are solemnly astonished at the bewildering allusions of the Irishman to a variety of mythical and historical Irish figures. The Second Workman, deeply conscious of his aristocratic pedigree, is particularly conscious of Ireland's mythology, and constantly refers to figures from the Irish past: the Grey of Macha, Cuchulain's horse, Nuad of the Silver Hand, whose amputated hand was replaced by a silver one, Fergus, the Fianna, Finn Mac Coole, Lugh of the Long Hand, the Sword of Light, Heber's children, Wolfe Tone, Shane the Proud, Parnell, Ormond, Offally, and the Dagda, all from legend or history, figure in the play, and most of them are mentioned by the Second Workman.

As in the other "visionary" play, *Red Roses for Me*, where the picture is of a dream world rather than of the real Ireland, there is throughout the play a significant awareness of Ireland's past greatness, underlined by continued references to her glorious past and mythology. "The Irish themselves know that they are the spiritual descendants of pioneers of Christian expansion, a source-nation of Western Culture. No matter how far they may have fallen from their earlier glory, they remember that their forebears once helped to civilize Europe," Blanshard says.[5] The Second Workman remembers that he is descended from the lords of Offally, who reigned "ere his ancient highness here was a thousand years from bein' born," and his assertion meets with no scorn from O'Casey but serves as an adequate reply to the condescension of Poges. It seems unfair that the Englishman's worship of the past should alone be satirized, as the common man probably fared as badly in the Ireland of Finn Mac Coole as in medieval England; nevertheless, the one is used as a symbol of glory, the other of capitalist ascendancy.

Another role of the Second Workman is that of the comic. With his fellows he relapses at times into knockabout farce, as in the disastrous episode with the quattrocento bureau. Yet another role is that of the romantic young lover, as he entices Souhaun from Poges and makes a fourth in the quartet with Avril and O'Killigain. It is he who first sees the rising river, and he is associated with O'Killigain in the highly symbolic dialogue in which the rising of the flood is noticed. Together the workers form a compact group against the two capitalists, and the women are immediately associated with the former; they themselves are Irish. They extort as much as possible from the two Englishmen before leaving them to their fate in the flood.

One of the main themes in the play is the satirical criticism of the unrealistic back-to-nature philosophy which, as already indicated, was an enthusiasm of Beverley Nichols, to whom Stoke bears a faint resemblance. It was also a fad of AE (George Russell), another whom O'Casey regarded as a poseur, insincere in philosophy and literature. He quotes Russell's opinion of cities as the last trap set for the spirit of man to draw him from nature and himself, and points out that there is as little of what Russell calls spirituality in the country as in the city. He describes Russell's account of the young man going back to nature in a large comfortable car, and it is to be remembered that

Poges builds a garage adjoining his Tudor mansion. He reduces the concept to its final absurdity by inquiring how much farther back one is to go—"To the skin-coat and the cave? To the tribe, or to the condition of feudal lord and feudal slave?" The "back to nature" theme is associated by O'Casey with the "back to the past" theme, and he deplores both as they imply a loss of all the modern advances in technology, medicine, and science, as well as the subjection of man to the overlord and the Church.

He points out that such a return is in any case impossible—man must go forward, and if there is a God, he is with the airplane in the sky just as much as he had been with the first ploughman who fixed a steel edge to his wooden plough.[6] O'Casey had had unhappy experiences in the country in a "horrible cottage" in Chalfont St. Giles, nineteen miles from London, with all the disadvantages of simple country life, and admits that "country life wasn't always lovely."

The Workmen clearly regard the rural affectations of Stoke and Poges as mad, and even Poges's high regard for Wordsworth, the arch poet of nature, is bitterly attacked by O'Killigain. Their purely literary and impractical knowledge is satirized even in their names, which come from the rural setting of Gray's "Elegy in a Country Churchyard," Stoke Poges. No sooner are they installed than Poges urgently requires a telephone to connect him with the city life which he proclaims he wishes to forget; both suffer miseries from the cold, from country noises, intrusive animals, and other natural dangers which they valiantly pretend to enjoy.

The position of the Church in the play is strikingly similar to the conception of materialistic clericalism which evolves in the later plays. Canon Creehewel is an indication that, even in this dreamlike comedy of unrealities, O'Casey is aware that all is not well with the real Ireland. The point is merely touched on here; in the later plays, Father Domineer, Canon Burren, and Father Fillifogue take up in detail the theme of the Church's alliance with materialistic capitalism in Ireland. Canon Creehewel admires the symbolic house; he approves of the past against the present; he accepts large gifts of money from Poges in return for which he obligingly turns a blind eye on the costumes of Avril and Souhaun. He opposes youth and gaiety, and criticizes O'Killigain for preventing his curate from punishing "a lasciviously-minded girl"—a brief picture which reminds us of Father Domineer and Loreleen in *Cock-a-Doodle Dandy*. He departs with the significant words, "I must be off . . . The soft rain that's falling may change to a downpour, and I've a long way to go"; he will be caught in the rising waters of the flood, like the capitalists with whom he associates.

The general picture is not intended to be a realistic account of contemporary Ireland. That is left for the later plays, and that is why, with *Red Roses for Me*, *Purple Dust* has been described as visionary. The Ireland here pictured is full of charming, humorous, entirely admirable Irish workers, all direct descendants of a noble race, without a care in the world, making fun of the foolish capitalists who wander into their clutches and affably relieving them of their money. There are signs of trouble, but O'Casey does not dwell on them.

On the whole it is one of the most lighthearted of his works. Only at the end is the gravity of the theme emphasized in the sinister appearance of the dark Figure, the retributive spirit of the rising flood, or in less symbolic terms the representative of socialism, which threatens the present structure of society. His language is symbolic: "Trees of an ancient heritage, that looked down on all below them, are torn from the power of the place they were born in, and are tossing about in the foaming energy of the waters."

From this it is clear that the theme of the play is not merely a frivolous comparison between Irish and English national characteristics; rather, like the themes of all his other plays, it springs from O'Casey's Socialist convictions, and in the vision he presents in symbolic terms a picture of what has not in fact yet come to pass: the sweeping away of capitalism and the past from which it grew and the triumph of the young workers who carry off the booty of their enemy as the latter is destroyed. In the next play he presents the same theme, the heroic efforts of the workers against capitalism, in a more serious and deeply moving manner.

9

A Tragic Vision

In *Purple Dust*, O'Casey had presented a dream world of Ireland showing the victory of socialism in symbolic guise against an uproariously comic background. In *Red Roses for Me* his subject is still the fulfillment of his dream of socialism triumphant, still set in a semi-ideal Ireland; but the vision is no longer comic. It concerns the strike of 1913, which had provided him with material for an earlier play, *The Star Turns Red*. However, while the latter dealt with concepts rather than characters, here he presents the theme in terms of real people who greatly resemble himself, his mother, and the friends of his early days. The play contains more autobiographical matter than any of the others and is also, perhaps consequently, among his best. The four main characters, Mrs. Breydon, the Reverend Mr. Clinton, Ayamonn, and Sheila, are lifted straight from O'Casey's account of his own experiences in his autobiography.

Mrs. Breydon is immediately identified with Mrs. Casside (O'Casey's mother) by her association with the three plants, musk, fuchsia, and geranium, which had provided the latter with her only glimpse of color in the dismal slum where she spent her life. It is at these that Mrs. Breydon looks anxiously after the stone in the street has crashed through the window. Her bed, like Mrs. Casside's is an old horsehair sofa which was uncomfortable enough, according to O'Casey, to send ecstasy to a saint. Ayamonn's admiration of his mother's staunch acceptance of the hard-

ships of life has a close parallel with O'Casey's testi-
mony to the brave stoicism of Mrs. Casside, and
brings to mind an interesting speculation by Kenneth
Tynan, writing in *Time* on the plays of Brecht, where
he ponders the theory that men who adore their mothers lean toward the Left, whereas those who idolize
their fathers lean toward the Right. Wild as this speculation seems to be, it fits in with O'Casey's admiration of his mother and his Socialist principles. His
father, who died young, is rarely mentioned.

The Reverend Mr. Clinton is another reminiscence
of O'Casey's early days when the rector of his church,
Mr. Griffin, to whom *Pictures in the Hallway* is dedicated, did much to help the young man in his struggles against slum life and poverty. There is also a
reference, perhaps, to Mr. Griffin's predecessor, Mr.
Harry Fletcher, who was a "decent minister . . . that
had made a great conquest of Johnny" (O'Casey).[1]
He was obliged to leave his parish because of opposition to his High Church principles, a fact which recalls Mr. Clinton's conflict with Foster and Dowzard.
In the main, however, Mr. Clinton reminds us of Mr.
Griffin. He too was attacked by Orangemen, bigoted
Protestants who "thought they saw a romish gleam in
the white of his eye," and an incident described in
Pictures in the Hallway, in which they are voted out
of the vestry of his church by the efforts of O'Casey,
shows that Ayamonn's devotion to his minister and
the latter's enlightened, unbigoted attitude are based
on facts.[2] The church with which both clergymen are
associated is St. Barnabas, in the play ironically
adapted to St. Burnupus in reference to the Christian
doctrine of damnation. The accounts of both men, in
the autobiography and the play respectively, have sim-
ilarities: a neatly cut beard, handsome face, black suit,
green scarf.

The touch of green in the Rector's dress may be

significant. As has been seen, it is for O'Casey the color of life, and those who support the cause of life, youth, and joy are nearly all associated with it—in the present play, the young Singer and the three women after their transformation. The Rector is also associated with the daffodils, also symbolic of life—"they simply signify the new life that Spring gives," he says, and his church is surrounded by flowers and flooded with color from the stained-glass windows. Like Mr. Griffin, he stands among those who, through kindness, wisdom, and toleration, are on the right side in the struggle of the oppressed against the oppressor.

Ayamonn is very clearly associated with O'Casey himself. He struggles to bring into his life as much color, art, and beauty as circumstances will allow; his belief that the pursuit of joy is the true way to worship God recalls the personal creed of O'Casey developed in *Within the Gates*; he is seen rehearsing the very play (*Henry VI*), in which O'Casey was to have acted with his brothers; even the costume is similar to that described in the autobiography, including a crimson cloak and a hat with a feather in it. He agonizingly hoards his coppers to buy a Constable reproduction, and longs, as O'Casey himself did, to paint well. His unorthodox attempts to increase his store of books nearly land him in jail, reminiscent of O'Casey's more successful theft of *Paradise Lost*. Like O'Casey, his awareness of beauty only makes him more keenly anxious to bring this and more material benefits to the common people; as has been seen, in the 1913 strike O'Casey was a keen supporter of Larkin: "Sean had come at last to hear Larkin speak, to stand under a red flag rather than the green banner."

Outside Ayamonn's window, the railway signal is visible as a constant reminder of his support of the Transport and General Workers' Union strike. Like

O'Casey, he owes allegiance to the labor cause rather than the national, as is seen by his refusal to follow Rory, who leaves the workers on the bridge in disgust. Nevertheless he is not unsympathetic to the latter's enthusiasm for the "Sword of Light," symbol of the Gaelic League, and it is a Celtic cross that he presents to the Rector.

Nora Creena, the young O'Casey's sweetheart, whose father and mother were against her having anything to do with him, figures in the play as Sheila, who is persecuted by the hostility of her parents to Ayamonn and is in fact poorly equipped with courage to defy the fierce respectability of her family. Like Sheila, who attends the retreat of St. Frigid in preference to keeping her appointment with Ayamonn, she is deeply superstitious and hostile to O'Casey's Communist and rationalist philosophy. Though finding pleasure in her company, in moments when she became "a red, red rose," just as Ayamonn did with Sheila, a "bonnie rose, delectable and red," he writhed under the necessity of having to dodge down a side-street to avoid meeting Nora's sister, until he realized that Nora wasn't the girl for him. "Not for Nora the charm of embroidered cloths under her feet, but the firmness of well-glazed oilcloth or the softness of a carpet . . . Not the red rose . . . for her swan-white breast, but a black cross, nestling chill and steady there." She is as unsuited to O'Casey as Sheila to Ayamonn, and in the play and the autobiography the lovers at last go their separate ways. In *The Plough and the Stars,* Nora Clitheroe had tried to make a stand against her husband's sacrifice of himself to an ideal and had been portrayed sympathetically; the scales are weighted against Sheila by the fact that the Nationalist cause of 1916 for which Jack Clitheroe fought was not in truth so near to O'Casey's heart as the struggle of the workers against the employers, and like the deaths of Jack and Drishogue, Ayamonn's martyrdom to the cause is thoroughly approved. Sheila is left with the thought that "roses red were never meant for me," and that she has failed Ayamonn.

The symbol of the roses is a complex one. In general it appears to represent the higher qualities of the human spirit—courage, manliness, vigor, integrity, love of art, all of which qualities are obscured in the workers by their drab lives, as the roses are half-hidden in the shawl. There is, too, a suggestion of sacrifice in the symbol—Sheila refuses to sacrifice herself for the cause—red roses are not for her—but a bunch of red roses is laid on the dead body of Ayamonn. His comment to Sheila may explain some of the significance of the symbol: "My feet shall be where the redder roses grow, though they bear long thorns, sharp and piercing, thick among them." The vision of a better life with consequent development of great human qualities can only be achieved by sacrifice, just as the beauty of the roses also implies the pain of the thorns.

As the title suggests, the symbol is at the core of the play, and it is developed in various ways. The visual image is of red roses half-hidden in a dark background. It reminds us of Ayamonn's efforts at creating beauty in the dark depths of the slum by bringing into his life art and drama. It reminds us of the apparently materialistic Brennan, whose drab preoccupation with money covers a bright spark of human compassion. It reminds us, too, of the dull colors of the statue which brighten into gleaming brilliance after its renovation. It reminds us most of all of the hidden potentialities of vigor, color, and noble sacrifice for the worker's cause. Throughout the play, as a leitmotiv, runs this contrast of the dark and the bright, the various implications gathered together under the symbol of the roses and the shawl.

The noticeable contrast between Ayamonn's surroundings and the bright clothes he wears while rehearsing indicates the truth of the first interpretation of the symbol, and the colorful energy of the Shakespearean lines similarly contrasts with the colloquial coarseness of Brennan's words which follow them, "Is anyone in or out or what?"

Brennan o' the Moor, a money-grubbing old miser, also reminds us that within the darkness of materialistic mind a hint of better things can lurk. He is anxious about the fate of the Bank of Ireland, since he has amassed money there at 4 per cent interest, and he is a slum landlord, yet his charity to little Ursula and the secret transformation of the statue indicate that he is no mere Ralph Nickleby, and with his music he is associated also with the attempt to brighten up the slums.

The transformation of the statue is a highly important symbol, and the change from its dull dirty condition to gleaming brightness is parallel to the image of the roses emerging from the darkness of the shawl. The dingy state of the statue is significant in view of the following lines: "She is wearing a crown that, instead of being domed, is castellated like a city's tower, resembling those of Dublin; and the pale face of the Virgin is sadly soiled by the grime of the house." The bedraggled figure, the "Lady of Eblana's poor," is in fact Dublin herself, before the transformation which takes place during the vision of the second act.

The men and women who venerated the statue are as pale and inanimate as the statue itself, their masklike faces still wearing a frozen look of resignation.

Their qualities also have to be developed, like the beauty of the statue. Yet no such easy transformation is possible for Eblana's poor as has come by kindly subterfuge to their lady; the great transformation which forms the peak of the play has to be fought and died for before it can take place; a miracle is wrought, not by trickery but by human effort and endurance.

The fourth interpretation of the symbol is the main theme of the play. The darkness of which the young Singer sings, and out of which the roses of sacrifice are to come, lies heavily upon the poor whom we see lounging helplessly on O'Connell Bridge. Their dark, lethargic misery is no figment of the imagination. W. P. Ryan describes it.

> If there is anything more depressing than a study of Dublin's slums in detail, it is a study of Dublin's slum dwellers in crowds, as when a national procession that represents some living and hopeful idea passes nearer the poorer quarters. The inertia and weariness and cold, clammy hopelessness of those street and wayside crowds make an awesome contrast.[3]

The conditions under which the people represented by the three women and their neighbors exist is documented by an overwhelming mass of evidence, as has been seen in the discussion of the first three plays. The Dublin slum dwellers live on a subhuman level; the remark of the Inspector, "Home with you, you lean rats, to your holes and haunts," is echoed by the *Irish Independent* in a leading article: "Out from the reeking slums, the jailbirds and most abandoned creatures of both sexes have poured, to vent their hatred upon their natural enemies, the police."[4]

The overcrowding and lack of privacy is one of the worst trials, as we have seen, of tenement life. Ayamonn, trying to study, has no peace from the intrusion of his neighbors; Sheila's unsuccessful attempts to gain admittance have, as she bitterly remarks, been viewed by a malicious audience of the neighbors, and her conversation with Ayamonn is unceremoniously interrupted by Brennan.

The poor in the play all bear witness by their appearance to the drabness of their lives. The pale, masklike faces of the women and the young Singer, the gray and brown clothes of the workers (with, however, bright patches of color somewhere about them, indicating the potentialities which are to be developed) are all significant. As the workers lounge on O'Connell Bridge, though the sun lights up the other parts of the scene there is no sign of sun where these people are. Eeada, Dympna, and Finnoola sit draped in black, so that they appear to be enveloped in the blackness of a dark night. The solid mass of the poor—sunless, dark, wretched, sleepy with indifference to life—these are the darknesses of which the Singer sings. These are the people for whom Ayamonn makes his sacrifice. They are the great, unindividualized mass for which he fights to bring courage and manliness; the darkness of their lives is the darkness of the shawl which hides the roses.

Yet, "throughout the Irish workers' world, in general we can see the association of stagnation and restlessness, pessimism and resurgence, gloom and gleam," W. P. Ryan says.[5] Art is beginning to spring among the masses; the young Singer sings his song, plays are being performed, and a gradual revitalizing of the scene is taking shape.

The workers' lives are soon to be illuminated, moreover, by the sacrifice of Ayamonn, under whose leadership they are to rise from their miserable state. Ayamonn is throughout the instrument of the resurgence. It is he who is the manager of the minstrel show, who writes the theme song, and who encourages the young Singer. He is the illuminating element through whom all the gloomy surroundings take on a new light. It is he who urges on the workers of Dublin and points out to them that "Meanness, spite, and common patth-erns are woven thick through all her glory; but her glory's there for open eyes to see." Their potentialities are as clear to him as the red roses hidden beneath the shawl, and he tries to make them see with his eyes: "The apple grows for you to eat. The violet grows for you to wear. Young maiden, another world is in your womb."

The response is timorous at first, as they think of the powers ranged against them, the police who will not hesitate to use their batons and arrest any they can lay their hands on. Yet Ayamonn bids them to take courage from the beauty of their city: "Take heart of grace from your city's hidden splendour," he says, pointing out the central theme of the play. The city is transfigured suddenly in the light of the setting sun and, with it, symbolically, the city's people; the three women rise from the black, shapeless shawls with new life, clothed in white and green; the third man begins to realize the truth of Ayamonn's message and says, "Our tired heads have always haunted far too low a level"; and the climax comes as Ayamonn and Finnoola dance in honor of the new resurgence of life and hope in Dublin.

An almost identical scene is described in *Pictures in the Hallway*, as the young O'Casey gazes entranced at the city bathed in the light of the sunset. He too feels the uplifting effect of the scene, for he resolves "to be strong; to stand out among many; to quit himself like a man."

To the tune of the hurdy-gurdy he dances with a young woman in and out of colored light as Ayamonn did with Finnoola, and he leaves her with the same words.[6] The spirit of exaltation is reinforced in the play by continual references to figures of Gaelic mythology, indicating that the debased figures of the poor are reverting to their ancient nobility: "Sons an' daughters of princes are we all, an' one with th' race of Milesius!" Finnoola earlier chose as her ideal the young Irish rebel, whose shabbiness was "threaded with th' colours from the garments of Finn Mac Cool of th' golden hair, Goll Mac Morna of th' big blows, Caoilte of th' flyin' feet, an' Oscar of th' invincible spear." Spanish ale and papal wine, promised by Mangan as symbols of Irish deliverance from the English in his song "The Dark Rosaleen," will, in Ayamonn's prophecy, soon foam on every hand and be a common drink—the common people will share in thy glorious future that is ahead. Ayamonn is continually associated with light and music, in this scene as at the end, when lights blaze around his body and Brennan's melodeon plays the song he wrote.

Yet the vision is not to be acquired cheaply. The sound of marching feet interrupts the dancers; the glory must be fought for before the workers can be transfigured like the statue, like Dublin itself, and Ayamonn leaves Finnoola to go and fight for the shilling in which, as Sheila says, he perhaps saw the shape of a new world.

This transformation which O'Casey poetically presents in the play did in fact take place. R. M. Fox asserts that Larkin's personal influence was almost miraculous.

> Men who were so broken and crushed that they would never have dreamt of making a stand, felt a new thrill of manhood in Larkin's presence. Everywhere the spirit of Labour quickened and long-repressed feelings of discontent stirred to life.[7]

Ryan repeats the idea: "The commonest of the 'common people' had at last seen a gleam and begun to follow it."

The historical incident which is the outcome of the transformation scene in Act III was the Transport and General Workers' Trade Union strike, which has been mentioned in the discussion of *The Star Turns Red*. An account of the whole story is to be found in the writings of James Connolly in the *Workers' Republic* and in Arnold Wright's *Disturbed Dublin*, the first in defense of the workers, the second for the employers.

The causes of the strike were the conditions of life and work of the Dublin workers. Throughout the writings of Connolly it is stressed that the strike, though paving the way for the 1916 Nationalist conflict by demonstrating the use of violent action, was brought about by economic conditions rather than national feeling.

In an attempt to counteract Larkin's weapon of the sympathetic strike and his doctrine of "tainted goods," the employers issued an ultimatum to the workers: Renounce Larkinism or go. O'Casey describes his own dismissal when he refused to obey this order. The growing unrest came to a head in the famous clash of the police and workers at a meeting in O'Connell Street. Like that to which Ayamonn was summoned, it had been proscribed by the authorities, and Larkin was arrested. It was then that the terrible occurrences described by O'Casey took place; the crowd was charged and batoned by mounted police and many were seriously injured, some killed.

These are the events which take place offstage in Act IV. The Inspector is based on the character of the Orangeman Edward Doosard, a vestryman and inspector of Quay police, who opposed Griffith. He sets the note by warning Ayamonn that "When swords are drawn and horses charge, the kindly Law, so fat with hesitation, swoons away, and sees not, cares not what may happen." In the actual event the behavior of the police, according to O'Casey's account, seems to have exceeded their legal rights, and in *Drums Under the Windows*, the third volume of the autobiography, he describes graphically some of the injuries suffered by innocent people. It is this scene from which the workers come streaming back during the fourth act in the play, and here that Dympna was wounded like the victim of the sabre cut whom O'Casey tried to help. Eeada's comment, "An' all along o' followin' that mad fool, Breydon," is a close parallel to the cry of a man in *Drums Under the Windows*: "We should never ha' listened to Larkin!" The Inspector, with his brutal indifference to the poor, his gaudy uniform, and his open threat of illegal assault in the event of a strike, indicates O'Casey's own view of the police, shared by Mrs. Breydon, who warns her son of the unpopularity of the police and the danger of associating with the daughter of a Royal Irish Constabulary sergeant.

In view of this, it is not surprising that scabs, or blacklegs, were the object of bitter scorn and derision, and the contemptible Foster and Dowzard are fair examples of the type.

The terrible consequences of the strike, the privation suffered by the workers and their families, are amply documented, the feelings of most being expressed in AE's famous "Open Letter to the Masters of Dublin." The apparent failure of Ayamonn in the failure of the strike was, however, misleading. At its close, labor was no longer an obscure, unregarded slave element. It had been in some measure, taking into consideration the psychological effects upon the reanimated workers, a drawn battle. The vision had not been completely achieved, but they had taken steps toward it.

Thus the historical background of the play, the resurgence of the working class in the strike of 1913, is expressed symbolically by the poetic conception of the roses hidden beneath the black shawl.

The bitterness of the class war is equalled by the religious animosity between Catholic and Protestant, a constant source of bitterness in Irish life, glimpsed in *The Shadow of a Gunman* and in *The Plough and the Stars*. In the present play, O'Casey shows that both religions can be narrow and bigoted when taken to extremes.

The Orangemen, or Northern Protestants, whose name came from the support given by the Protestants to William of Orange in his struggle with the deposed Catholic James II, had rules of exclusion as strict as the Catholic rules on mixed marriage. No Catholic or Jew might belong to an Orange order, and if an Orangeman married a Catholic he was immediately dropped from any Orange order to which he belonged. Mrs. Breydon warns Ayamonn that marriage must be regulated by the faith of the woman and the man concerned, and she is fearful of praising the statue: "She's not a thing for Protestant eyes to favor."

Sheila's parents are bitterly hostile to her association with a Protestant, and she herself is fearful of breaking rules when in the grounds of St. Burnupus. In contrast, Ayamonn stands above such narrowness by his open-minded toleration of the superstitions of the poor Catholics, the free-thinking Mullcanny, and the Protestant bigotry of Brennan. Foster and Dowzard are the representatives of Orangeism at its worst. They are reflections of the narrow vestrymen at the church of St. Burnupus under the Reverend Mr. Griffin, who are voted out of office by the efforts of

O'Casey in *Pictures in the Hallway*. They seize on the cross as an emblem of popery and view the labor disputes as an attack on their religion. Even the old verger, Samuel, grunts a criticism of the Rector, who had given permission for the lights to be left on in the church where Ayamonn lay.

Other aspects of the contemporary scene are found in the appearance of the Irish Irelander, Roory O'Balacaun. The faults here satirized are those of stupidity and an exclusive nationalism which can see no further than the green flag. The character is based partly on the character of O'Casey's friend the tram conductor, who was blinded by his enthusiasm for the national cause to the sufferings of the poor. O'Casey tried to interest his friend in Ruskin's *Crown of Wild Olive* in a conversation which is the origin of indentical lines in the play, but he is blind to all colors but green and criticizes the book because it is not Irish. Ayamonn in the parallel incident tries to explain to Roory the international creed of Socialism: "Irish or English—[it's all] th' same"; but Roory disagrees, for "we have th' light," he says. The light he speaks of is not the Catholic faith, but the Sword of Light, the symbol of the Gaelic League, his only guide, and he is anxious to drag Ayamonn from the workers on the bridge. Yeats speaks of "the ignorant sort of Gaelic propagandist, who would have nothing said or thought that is not in country Gaelic. One knows him without trouble. He writes the worst English and would have us give up Plato and all the sages for a grammar." Rory is a good example.

Throughout the play he is a figure of fun. Wearing the trench coat that was the favorite garment of the Republicans, he carries his Irish magazines in much the same way as Mullcanny waves his *Riddle of the Universe*. He criticizes the minstrel show, absurdly, as being unpatriotic; he protests against the casual mention of a royal command, and his puritanism asserts itself uneasily at what he thinks is indecency in the young Singer's song. He is a member of one of the puritanical young men's societies which were a favorite butt of O'Casey, and is held up for ridicule when, good Catholic as he is, he adopts the position of a Mohammedan at prayer to avoid the stones thrown through the window. Yet O'Casey does not ignore the potential danger of his type, and Ayamonn admonishes him, "If we give no room to men of our time to question many things, all things, ay, life itself, then freedom's but a paper flower." The comment is interesting in view of O'Casey's later attitude to the Ireland of reality depicted in the later plays.

Mullcanny the rationalist is another old friend. He appeared as the Covey in *The Plough and the Stars* and as the Atheist and the Man with the Stick in *Within the Gates*. Again O'Casey delights in the squabbles of the rationalist, with his scientific catchwords ("os coccyges"), against the Catholic Roory, with whom the Protestant Brennan uneasily sides against the free-thinking foe until the old quarrels of "King Billy," the Pope, and the Battle of the Boyne break out again. His present occupation is significant in view of the growing snobbery which was to be satirized in the later plays; he spends his time "Hammering knowledge into deluded minds wishing to be civil servants."

The hostility between him and Roory is shadowed in the autobiography where O'Casey describes the fulminations of St. Laurence O'Toole against any questioning of the literal interpretation of Genesis, and shows how he himself acquired knowledge, by the help of Frazer's *Golden Bough* and Shaw's works, of the true story of man's struggle to his present level.

Mullcanny and O'Balacaun are well-balanced. Neither is intelligent enough to be more than a mechanical mouthpiece of the creed he represents, and each is a recognizable figure of the Ireland of his time.

Although these contemporary figures and references are present in the play, however, the impression is one of vision rather than an accurate mirror of actual events. As in *Purple Dust*, the chief characters move in the splendor of their ancient traditions and the plays are linked by the consciousness of glorious feats and ancient heroes which emphasizes the visionary qualities of both plays, the comic *Purple Dust* and the tragic *Red Roses for Me*. The heroes disappear in the next group of plays. In the real Ireland, which O'Casey now turns to consider for the first time since *The Plough and the Stars*, there is little enough to remind him of ancient Celtic glories.

10

Contemporary Ireland — The Reality

In *The Bishop's Bonfire*, Father Boheroe advises young Keelin and Daniel, "You've escaped from the dominion of the big house with the lion and unicorn on its front; don't let yourselves sink beneath the meaner dominion of the big shop with the cross and shamrock on its gable." It is O'Casey's concern with the possibility of this fate overtaking Ireland which led him to turn his attention in three plays, *The Bishop's Bonfire*, *Cock-a-Doodle Dandy*, and *The Drums of Father Ned*, from upholding the cause of socialism to an examination of the Ireland which emerged from the violence and upheaval of rebellion and civil war over thirty years ago, and which he had long neglected in favor of world affairs.

As he had foreseen before his departure, the Ireland of the present, after struggling for centuries against political oppression and freeing herself by superhuman effort from British control, had meekly succumbed to the power of commercial materialism under the benevolent supervision of the Church. In these three plays, O'Casey pitilessly satirizes the chief curses of the present-day Ireland, mercenary narrowness of mind, killjoy pietism, and hypocritical lipservice to ideals of nationalism long in fact disregarded. The struggle between those who support the Irish way of life described above and the young at heart who oppose it is visualized as having various solutions, different in each play, but it is always in effect the same struggle. The solution offered in *Cock-a-Doodle Dandy* is defeatist. Ireland is beyond spiritual salvation and all that is good, young, and vigorous in the land in the persons of Loreleen and the Cock, a facet of her personality, depart, leaving behind an island of old men. In *The Bishop's Bonfire*, the solution is even more pessimistic; the young remain, to be crushed by the forces against them, and are themselves affected by the prevailing timorousness and pietism and suffer accordingly. Daniel loses his chance for happiness with Keelin, and Foorawn loses her life through her self-willed rejection of life and love. In *The Drums of Father Ned*, however, a new note is sounded. One of the decorations used in the festival bears the words, "We were Dead and are Alive Again!" This, in effect, is the theme of the play. A new life springs into being; Ireland is flooded with music, poetry, and young love; the philistine capitalists and narrow parish priests are beaten into subjection by the victorious young people.

In *The Bishop's Bonfire* contemporary Ireland is symbolically pictured in the miserable state of Reiligan's land, with its lean cattle, thin milk, worn-out meadows giving dusty hay, with no fine buildings, no color, no thought. The Codger says there is no heart in the soil, no heart in the grass that tops it: "Hay? Dust that the weary cattle can't chew. There isn't a sign in any meadow even of clover or of vetch . . ." while the cattle complain silently to God against the beginning of another day. The agricultural barrenness is actual as well as symbolical; O'Casey points out in *The Green Crow* that the Codger's remarks are based on fact. Nevertheless it provides a useful parallel to the spiritual state of the land. The dry, bitter images are echoed by the withering of young life in Ireland. In *Cock-a-Doodle Dandy* the land is emptied of the young, who retreat from the place where "a whisper of love . . . bites away some of the soul," and those who are left are dying spiritually as Julia is dying physically. Michael is told at the end of the play, "Die. There is little else left useful for the likes of you to do." The fate of the young who are caught in this dying land is terrible. They will become "but dusty questions that life has never answered," and no young life will spring from them. The ashes left by the celebration bonfire for the Bishop are symbolical of the dead love of the four young people; the emphasis is continually on dust, ashes, and barrenness, and those who are left are condemned to a life empty of love and joy.

There is an overwhelming mass of evidence for the generally depressing state of affairs which O'Casey thus presents by selected images, and for which nearly all contemporary Irish writers have expressed their concern. The lack of social activities, the unnatural restriction on young people, the opposition to social reform in medicine and in child welfare, petty taboos and tyrannies, and corrupt politicians are among the dangers which many Irish writers see besetting their native land. The visitor may get the impression of a prosperous, well-to-do country, writes Sean O'Faoláin in "Ireland After Yeats," but beneath the surface "such things as emigration, a falling population, frustrated lives which are so evident in late and too few marriages, the thinning countryside" indicate a less happy picture. "Contemporary Irish society [is] acquisitive, bourgeois, unsophisticated, intellectually conservative, and unadventurous, rigidly controlled by a church which is at once loved and feared."

The lonely old men at the end of O'Casey's play are not merely figments of his imagination, for "Dr. Clement S. Mihanovitch . . . reaches the conclusion that Ireland is rapidly becoming a nation of a meager handful of old men and women." [1] The picture of a land where freedom is restricted by clerical vigilance, the young people thwarted, crushed into submission or banished, the arts suspected and severely censored, and the whole outlook one of bourgeois philistinism motivated by the desire to make money, is frequently presented in the writings of modern Irishmen and especially in these three plays of O'Casey.

James Joyce diagnosed the trouble. In Ireland, "Christ and Caesar are hand in glove." The Codger puts his finger on the same thing. "Oh! the Canon's voice! The Church an' State's gettin' together." he mockingly exclaims, and we are earlier told that Reiligan is the biggest moneyman of the district, a loyal pillar of the Church, and has a great power and influence in the affairs of the state.

O'Casey is repelled by the unholy alliance, and his indignation reached a climax when De Valera, as head of the Irish state, knelt to receive the blessing of a visiting cardinal, which O'Casey regarded as a humiliating thing for the head of a republican state to do, but he reflects bitterly that Ireland was no longer a republican state, either in theory or in practice—"she was a theocracy, fashioned by the Vatican, and decked in the brightest sacerdotal array by the bishops of Maynooth." [2]

The evidence for the truth of O'Casey's point of view is overwhelming, and he himself vigorously defends the accuracy of the picture he has drawn in these plays. To the charge that "the Ireland of the young O'Casey is dead," he retorts in *The Green Crow* with a devastating account of the Irish bishops' interference with social reform when they "tore the Mother and Child Bill straight in two," describing also the poor services in elementary schools for children's meals, the puritanical censorship of books and films, and referring the still dubious reader to the "hundreds of instances of clerical control given in *The Irish and Catholic Power*."

In the latter, Paul Blanshard points out that the Irish

> permit ecclesiastical dictatorship and political democracy to live side by side without any sense of incongruity . . . the Irish priests have . . . a program for the control of great areas of modern life which belong to democracy, such general areas as elementary education, freedom of thought, domestic-relations law, and medical hygiene; and such specific political areas as Irish Partition, Franco's fascism, Jerusalem's independence, and Tito's collaboration with the West. On all these issues Irish bishops and priests . . . carry their moral authority over into the world of citizenship and tell their people what they should and should not do.[3]

The results of this, Blanshard feels, have been disastrous, for Irish policy on church and state has produced in Southern Ireland "a society where cultural freedom and, to a certain extent, genuine political freedom have been sacrificed to clerical dictatorship."[4] Sean O'Faolain points out that in Ireland the Hierarchy does more than comment or advise; it commands, he says, and the "lightest word from this quarter is tantamount to the raising of the sword. . . . The Dail proposes; Maynooth disposes." O'Casey himself quotes Dr. Lucey as saying that the Hierarchy of Ireland are the final arbiters of right and wrong even in political matters, and mentions the remark of a Holy Ghost Father at a meeting of Regnum Christi on October 31, 1955, who said that while some well-educated Catholics think it is fashionable to question and contradict in private, and even in public, the teaching and decisions of the bishops, this merely showed how ill-instructed many Catholics were in elementary Christian duty—obedience, for it belonged to the bishops alone to decide both where the limits of their authority extended and in what measure to exercise it. Constitutionally the Catholic Church holds a special position in the state, and as freedom of conscience and free profession of religion are guaranteed to every citizen, subject only to public order and morality, the arbiters of such morality usually prove to be the leaders of the Church, who interpret it in the light of Catholic policy. Ireland is a country, says O'Faolain, where "the policeman and the priest are in a perpetual glow of satisfaction."

Thus the presentation of Ireland as a state strongly dominated by the power of the Church is well authenticated. In the plays, the power of the Church and its place in the land are immediately indicated by significant touches. The house of Michael Marthraun is bedecked with papal colors, by a great clump of yellow sunflowers and twisted pillars of white wood, significantly contorted out of normal lines, a little on the skew. Beyond the house of Councillor Reiligan the skyline of the town is dominated by its highest building, the church, in the manner of the great spire seen through the window in *The Star Turns Red*. Within the house, the same theme is continued by the two lampshades, one white, one yellow, and the yellow and white stripes round the tub carried in by Rankin. Even in the "prerumble" of *The Drums of Father Ned*, the scene has its appropriate ecclesiastical symbol—the Celtic cross, dazzling in its whiteness, which stands a little crookedly in the Irish street.

The official policy of the Church represented by these symbols has already been touched upon in discussing the power of the Church in the Irish state. It is, in the main, reactionary in all spheres, particularly in the area of social reform, so dear to O'Casey. Many examples of the attitude against which O'Casey was protesting may be cited. The British *Report on Population* (1949), a serious and enlightened work, was described by the *Irish Catholic* as having the morals of a stud farm (June, 1949); in the same issue the editor protested against the possibility of Ireland entering the non-Catholic organization of U.N.O.; in the same year, a meeting of the literary and historical society of University College, Dublin, which was to have a discussion on the one hundred-year-old *Communist Manifesto* of Marx and Engels, was cancelled by the president of the college, who later told an official of the Irish Association of Civil Liberties that the students were not allowed to choose freely what would be discussed inside the walls of the college. Other reactionary views of the Church are exemplified in the opposition to sex education in schools; the policy of teaching all subjects from a specifically Catholic point of view; and disloyalty to the state on the matter of income-tax returns (*Irish Times*, May 23, 1953). These are random instances where a fuller study would be out of place, but they are to some extent indicative of the general policy of the Church in Ireland.

It is the unenlightened attitude of the Church to the worker, however, which especially rouses O'Casey's indignation. The encyclical *Rerum Novarum* is a particular object of his satire, as has been seen in the study of *The Star Turns Red*. In the dedication of *The Drums of Father Ned* he speaks warmly of Father Yorke of San Francisco, who warned Dr. McDonald, his friend, that in *Rerum Novarum* the Church was offering the workers no more than a string of platitudes. Marthraun, the capitalist, however, feels that its support is welcome in his dealings with his workmen. To the Second Rough Fellow's demand, "Tell me how I'm goin' to live a week on tuppence," he replies "That's a social question to be solved by th' Rerum Novarum." Father Fillifogue says he is hoarse trying to teach his flock the right way to look at the Church's social teachings, but its philosophy, to O'Casey's mind, is little more than a bulwark of capitalism. Now, to his satisfaction, the workers are no longer overawed by the capitalist doctrine that "when they work for us they're workin' for God," or as Canon Burren puts it, "when you are working for the Councillor, Rankin, however menial the job may be, you are serving God."

Throughout these plays the Church is consistently associated with capitalism. Father Domineer's main preoccupation is in fighting what he considers to be the sexual laxity of the people, but he is closely associated with Mahan and Marthraun and is significantly anxious about the former at the hands of the crowd which has maltreated Loreleen; Canon Burren is rarely seen out of the company of Reiligan, and Father Fillifogue is left at the end of *The Drums of Father Ned* in a stupefied condition with his two capitalistic friends.

The general tendency of the Church to encourage meekness and crawling piety in the working man enraged O'Casey, and a glance at *Matt Talbot, Alcoholic*, by Father Albert H. Dolan, convinces us that he had some ground for his feeling. Father Dolan speaks approvingly of Talbot's abstention from all political attempts to better the position of the working classes, and of the masochistic penances he inflicted upon himself as a result of which he dropped dead on a Dublin Street. O'Casey meets this with scorn, and asks satirically of the workingman, "Why do you look for a comfortable home with light and heat and colour in it? You fools! Consider Matt Talbot and you'll realise that these poor things are but vanity." Though Talbot is not mentioned by name in these plays, the attitude which he represented, a pious rejection of material goods which made him for his employers a model workman and for his fellow workers a traitor to his class, is continually condemned. It is this attitude, by which the Church encourages otherworldliness in the workers for the benefit of the capitalist, that O'Casey censures in these plays.

This alliance of the Church with capitalism and the attempt to lead the workers into accepting poor social conditions is closely allied with the mercenary attitude of the clergy. This point, noted in *Purple Dust*, is dwelt upon with much bitterness in *The Bishop's Bonfire*, though the sardonic note is also sounded in *Cock-a-Doodle Dandy*, when the Messenger exclaims that honor by the clergy is regulated by how much a man can give. The mockery becomes more bitter in the later play; Canon Burren is a smaller, meaner figure than the sinister Domineer, and his anxious money-grubbing lacks even the dignity lent by terror. Where the one is burly, heavily built, Burren is short, plump, awkward, his legs seeming to trot when he walks. He is a comic figure, yet his materialistic nature is at once emphasized by the coarse, heavy set of his face. His objection to spending money which might otherwise go into the Church funds on roses at once clarifies his ideas on life generally, for in *Red Roses for Me* we have seen that these flowers symbolize for O'Casey the higher qualities of the human spirit.

Burren tries to persuade the Codger, on the other hand, that Reiligan's poor-quality hay is good; he is delighted with the honor done the capitalist when the Councillor becomes a count, and is careful to treat him with scrupulous politeness. Manus, toward the

end of the play, also speaks of the unholy collaboration, and he sardonically comments upon how readily
the Canon would bless any place where money lay.
The satirical little play *Time to Go* echoes the same
theme: "This pinchin' be th' priests of th' little we
have is gettin' unconthrollable." Ireland is "Priest-puf-
fin island . . . An' it's not a shillin' they want, or even
a half-a-crown; oh, no; th' mineemus now asked from
a poor thrader is a pound, if you please."

Father Fillifogue is less immediately concerned
with money in his struggle with Father Ned and the
Tostal—as Father Domineer exemplified the clerical
attitude to sex and Canon Burren the attitude to
money, Father Fillifogue's attention is almost exclusively concerned with art and the evils thereof, yet like
Canon Burren he displays characteristics which mark
him as both ludicrous and materialistic. He is baldish,
with tufts of gray hair protruding from beneath a soft
gray hat, his trousers are baggy, and a little short even
for his short legs, and at the same time the fleshy lines
of his face betray him—his head is round and broad,
his nose thick, and his mouth seemingly forever com-
pressed, the lips tightly closed in a mood of resigned
annoyance with the surrounding world.

This mercenary outlook of the clergy in general
leads to a narrow suspicion of all art, poetry, music,
and beauty in general. Father Domineer commands
the dancers to cease, and rants that "pagan poison is
floodin' th' world . . . Ireland is dhrinkin' in generous
doses through films, plays, an' books." He criticizes
the bright ornaments worn by Loreleen and tries to
burn her books, which include a volume about Vol-
taire and James Joyce's *Ulysses*. Burren too is a philistine, preferring money to roses, interrupting the dance
of Daniel and Keelin in the manner of Domineer, and
commenting viciously on the singing of the Codger.

Father Fillifogue, however, more than either of these two, is the archenemy of art and beauty. He tries to substitute for the music of Bach, Beethoven, Haydn, and Handel some artistically worthless hymns of his own choice and vigorously opposes the works of Mozart, so enthusiastically admired by Murray the choirmaster. Father Fillifogue interrupts the singing of the Tostal song in favor of a dreary hymn, and tries to impose his taste on the others. He is horrified at the bright colors of window boxes, doors, and lampposts decorated for the Festival, especially when his own door, with wicked irony, is painted "a flaming red."

The official expression of this attitude toward art in Ireland is the censorship of literature and, like other writers, O'Casey has protested bitterly against it. It is "prelatian-led crowd of ding dong dedero devotees, roaring out opposition to everything outside of what Father Tom, Dick, or Harry thought proper to be put in poem or book." [5] In *The Green Crow* he describes in detail the consistent opposition of the clergy to all forms of art and its consequent lapse in Ireland.[6]

The Constitution itself leaves a definite opening for official censorship: "The State shall endeavour to ensure that organs of public opinion such as the Radio, Press and Cinema . . . shall not be used to undermine public order or morality." The ambiguousness of the term morality allows a variety of interpretations and is usually held to mean Catholic views on this subject. In the *Irish Monthly*, Stephen J. Brown flatly claimed that neither art nor literature had any rights against the claims of God, while Canon 1399 of Church law asserts that books against God are those which of set purpose are concerned with obscene or impure topics, impugn or deride Catholic dogmas, attempt to overthrow ecclesiastical discipline, declare that dueling, suicide, or divorce are licit, aim to defame the Hierarchy or the clerical or religious state, defend heresy or schism, or attack religion or good morals. Dr. Cornelius Lucey, Bishop of Cork, speaking on Article 40 of the Constitution, which deals with the legal punishment of the publication or utterance of indecent matter, observed that while there was reason for state toleration of freedom of religious opinion, there was no reason for similar license to be offered to unbelief, or propaganda on behalf of it.

Protests against such an attitude are vigorous and bitter among Irish writers. Owen Sheehy Skeffington comments that in Ireland, ironically, a religion based on transcending love finds too often its expression in uncharitable and misinformed attacks on any who dare to hold differing views. The dramatist Paul Vincent Carroll regards official government censorship as foolish and pernicious, since it has handed over power to the puritan, an alien figure in Ireland's history. Even more pernicious, however, is the unofficial censorship which Carroll describes as being prevalent through rural areas where the local priest, sometimes old and crusty, sometimes young and inexperienced, bans some activity with a power against which there is no appeal, in order to safeguard an ignorance which is confused with natural innocence. O'Casey joins with these and many others in deploring that "a country where so many were never afraid to die is now a country where so many are afraid to live . . . Ireland's a decaying ark in western waters, windows bolted, doors shut tight, afraid of the falling rain of the world's thought." [7] The bitter contrast between Ireland's heroic past of national rebellion and her present degraded state of cautious, materialistic conservatism is a major theme among modern Irish playwrights, responsible for a good deal of the irony which runs through modern Irish literature.

The distrust of art is connected with the materialistic outlook of the three priests, but is also clearly connected with their suspicion of any manifestation of natural sexual feeling in the young people. The entire emphasis of *Cock-a-Doodle Dandy* is on the clerical attitude toward youth and love, and though this puritanism permeates the whole Irish scene as presented in the play, it is the priest who leads the way in condemning all that is young and vital in life. He is viciously opposed to Loreleen, the chief representative of these qualities, whom he regards as a "proud an' dartin' cheat," and he warns Marthraun to get rid of her. He approves the brutality of the crowd in dragging her before him, and provokes her into the significant outburst: "When you condemn a fair face, you sneer at God's good handiwork. You are layin' your curse, sir, not upon a sin, but on joy." She is banished, but with her the other gay young women and the young Messenger go, leaving behind the old people in a desolate scene.

The Bishop's Bonfire shows even more clearly the bitterness of frustration which results from this narrow attitude of the clergy. Canon Burren's first words express his disapproval of the association between Manus and Foorawn, and he is instrumental in separating Daniel and Keelin. He tries instead to promote an arranged match between Keelin and a middle-aged farmer for business reasons, and we remember the wretched marriage of Michael and Lorna in the earlier play. W. P. Ryan comments on the repellently materialistic marriages which take place in the Irish farming class, the outcome of matchmaking which he regards as human buying and selling. "The full tale of the Irish clerical war on lovers would make a big, strange volume of repression and adventure . . . their sure and shortsighted teaching on the subject of love, or rather their denunciation of it, has done much to blight and mar and materialise humanity in a deal of rural Ireland." [8]

It is clear from the above and many other references that O'Casey's view of the priest in Ireland, discouraging romantic love, suspicious of sex, and wholly materialistic, is as modern as he claims in *The Green Crow*, and certainly justifiable enough to be shared by many others. The effect of clerical activity on the Irish mentality will be discussed later. It is first important to establish that the priest has, as O'Casey claims, power to enforce his ideas. Nora outlines the power, as she defies it at the end of *The Drums of Father Ned*.

> You see, Father, we're fed up bein' afraid our shaddars'll tell what we're thinkin'. One fool, or a few, rules th' family life; rules th' school, rules th' dance hall, rules th' library, rules th' ways of a man with a maid, rules th' mode of a girl's dhress, rules th' worker in fields and factory, rules th' choice of our politicians, rules th' very words we try to speak, so that everything said cheats the thruth! an' Doonavale has become th' town of th' shut mouth.

In *Cock-a-Doodle Dandy* the power is shown by the generally submissive attitude of the people to Father Domineer. The one force which he cannot subdue is the power of money and business interests, and his order to Mahan to dismiss a good workman is ignored —Mahan, meek in all other things, refuses to budge on this issue. Otherwise the priest's power is complete. Burren is fully aware of his power and points out to Father Boheroe that "the love they may have for you doesn't come near the fear they have for Reiligan [*he pauses*] or the reverence they must show for their Parish Priest." O'Casey describes the new state of things in *Inishfallen, Fare Thee Well*.

Almost as long as Sean could remember, the life of Ireland was lived in a hall whose walls were roof-high stained-glass windows, nationally designed; but these were giving place now to glass that gave back the colours of pietistic twist and glossied tantrum. The window where Wolfe Tone had shone in his sky-blue coat and bright epaulettes of a Brigadier, now showed the wan figure of Bernadette raptly listening to the Bells of St. Mary's; in the one which had Robert Emmet [sic] in his gay green coat, carrying a plumed hat in his hand, stood now the black-clad, smiling-faced Father Malone is his new Sunday hat.[9]

He points out sadly that the great ideals of the Irish Republicanism which had kept alive for centuries have been warped, when at last put into practice, by the submission of the nation's leaders to the priests: "Ireland today shows the idea of Republicanism that filled the minds and hearts of the I.R.B. Remember, Republicanism overthrows, not only government by hereditary monarchy, but also government by clerical dictator; is purely a secular philosophy," he said in a letter to me, and in common with the great majority of Irish writers of today his attitude to the outcome of the centuries-long struggle for freedom is one of intense disillusionment.

The effect of the priest upon the life and attitude of the people is clearly seen in all three plays, for the strangling narrowness of Irish pietism emerges as the most prominent feature of the contemporary scene. In *Cock-a-Doodle Dandy* the two capitalists discuss the powers of evil and underline the theme of the play— that women are regarded as the devil incarnate by the sex-shy Irish—a race of men "whose abhorrence of their Christian, social, and racial duty has led them to persuade themselves that a natural impulse is an evil thing and that women are the devil's handiwork." [10]

O'Casey regards this as hilariously funny and weaves a whole fantastic fabric from the literal interpretation of the idea, yet the bitterness in the Irishman's mind is allowed full play, and to Mahan's protest that "there's nothin' evil in a pretty face, or in a pair of lurin' legs" Marthraun replies that "your religion should tell you th' biggest fight th' holy saints ever had was with temptations from good-lookin' women."

He exclaims that "there's evil in that woman," referring to his own young wife, for on looking at her reflection in the mirror, he had seen brightly colored horns branching from her head. She is a woman and young, and this is enough to make her a devil in the eyes of the Irishman, in more than a metaphorical sense. Shanaar also represents this warped aspect of the Irish mind; he feels that "women is more flexible towards th' ungodly than us men, an' well th' old saints knew it." The Sergeant of Police agrees that they will have to curtail the gallivanting of the women after men, and Michael repentantly remembers that St. Jerome once told a brother that woman was the gate of hell. Ryan, in *The Pope's Green Island*, comments that "Some Irish Catholic laymen . . . have yet a curious feeling when they come into opposition to the priests over social, educational or intellectual issues that they contend in a sense with occult and unknown. There is a touch of weirdness in the air . . . the priest is regarded in rural areas as a sacred magician who could turn obstreperous sinners into animals." [11]

This feeling is apparently shared by the priests and their supporters in the fight against the "evil forces," for there is more than a "touch of weirdness" in *Cock-a-Doodle Dandy*, where the tables are turned and the magic is on the other side. Loreleen, as a woman, is interchangeable with the gay, colorful, and vigorous Cock, who is regarded as an evil spirit by the pious characters, while the other women indicate their similar propensities by sprouting horns from time to time.

In *The Bishop's Bonfire*, the forces of gaiety and courage are represented by the Codger and Keelin, but they fight against heavy odds. Daniel's love for the latter is quickly doused by the authority of the Canon, and the Codger, though irrepressible, is dismissed. Foorawn, caught more deeply than any in the pietism that denies the value of earthly love and normal passions, shows more clearly than any the effects of this pernicious philosophy—she is the "mournful, empty shell of womanhood," a "sombre musk rose." The puritanism of the present hangs more heavily over Ireland than the poverty of the past. The sable shawl of which O'Casey speaks in the beginning of *The Drums of Father Ned* is perhaps significant; the "sober black shawl" of *Red Roses for Me* was in fact the dark misery of the Dublin slums—here it is the even more sinister shadow of spiritual deadness that overhangs Ireland.

Many writers deplore this prudery and suspicion of women, a wide selection of them being found in a collection of articles under the title of *The Vanishing Irish*, in which such writers as Maura Laverty, Arland Ussher, Mary Keating, and several others are in agreement with O'Casey's delineation of the Irish scene. One quotation may perhaps stand for all.

> The dismal fact remains that Irishmen tend to regard procreation as a shameful necessity, and Irish girls grow up to think of sex as something dark, cold, and forbidding. Statistics are scarcely available, but it seems to me that the word "dirty" is used in modern Ireland in one sense only, namely, to cover every manifestation, even the most natural, of sex passion.[12]

Mary Keating's observation that mothers would be happier to see all their sons and daughters become priests and nuns than see them mix with their own kind and seek salvation in the world at once recalls the attitude of Foorawn in the play.

O'Casey points out that frequently the Church has had this effect when in power; hence his bitter hatred of the Middle Ages, when the Church was all-powerful. Bitterly he sketches the state of Ireland today: "Women and war—two terrible dangers. Wherever she goes, rings on her fingers and bells on her toes, she trails behind her devotion that should go to God, destruction that should never come near Man."

In art as in life, the Irish mind is suspicious of possible temptations. Mahan exclaims "What do people want with books?" while the Sergeant considers them to be the biggest curse of all, and the Prodical gloats over the bonfire that is to burn up all the "bad" books in honor of the Bishop's visit. Father Fillifogue imagines that he has been successful in driving Nora from her position as librarian, and congratulates himself that the books chosen by her have been removed from the shelves. Such actions against liberally minded librarians must have been fairly common, and in the *Irish Times* of February 16, 1931, an article appeared in which the writer commented with satisfaction on the fact that the representatives of a Catholic people were unwilling to subsidize libraries not under Catholic control. Even apart from non-Catholics, he pointed out that not even all Catholics were fit to be in charge of a public library for Catholic readers, and concluded by saying that such an onerous position should be assigned to an educated Catholic who would be as remarkable for his loyalty to his religion as for his intellectual attainments.

Book, pictures, women, youth, all coalesce to form the enemy of the pietistic Irishman; yet, O'Casey points out, this Irishman is not sexless, but merely repressed. The point is emphasized by Dr. Patrick Hofferman in *The Liberal Ethic,* which claims that the Irish are not undersexed, but merely afraid of sex and everything sexual, even to the point of avoiding such evocative words as chastity, which they replace with purity. He feels that the Irish come close to being heretical Manichees or Gnostics, haters of nature and the beautiful, and blames their dread of sex for the low marriage rate and habit of marrying too late to have children. In a picturesque phrase he describes the Irish countryside as a place "full of middle-aged bachelors stalking like old billygoats through the land, and soured spinsters who make every Irish village a valley of squinting windows." Mahan and Marthraun are a fair example of what Dr. Hofferman is describing. Neither is hysterical, like Rankin, who would appear to be sexually abnormal—they show glimmers of normal feeling, flirt with Marion, and take part in the dance, before being recalled to penitence by their own superstitious fear of the priest.

The pietism of these Irish puritans is allied to their superstition. The major target in this field is the pathetic trust of sufferers in the miraculous powers of Lourdes, and Julia's departure and lonely return, uncured, indicate O'Casey's bitter reflections on the folly of it all. In *Inishfallen, Fare Thee Well* he speaks of

the orderly, money-making orgy of Lourdes, strange tinselled waste, and woeful issue of a sick child's slick dream; tipping rose-leaves out on running sores and eating cancers; setting its comic, codified cure, by dipping the sick into a well, thick with the scum of a thousand tumors, against the calmly measured scientific healing of millions, without the singing of a single psalm.[13]

In all the singing of the "Ave Maria," he hears beneath the hymn the bitter disillusioned cry of the disappointed—"she didn't cure me." Superstition is more amusingly satirized in the admonitions of Shanaar, who can calculate the number of evil spirits that can lodge under the skin of one man, and speaks with horror of the Widda Malone, who could turn herself into a dog or a hare. Throughout the play, the literal interpretation of figurative expressions is continually mocked, and O'Casey presents the spirit-ridden top hat, whiskey bottle, and exorcism scene with great gusto. Statues and their supposed powers offer him much amusement; in *Cock-a-Doodle Dandy* they shudder when Loreleen passes by, though the plaster saint in *The Bishop's Bonfire* is made of sterner stuff, and exerts a wary vigilance over the inhabitants of the house, terrifying all who displease him with blasts from his "buckineeno." Modern pietism moreover has become affected with a sentimentality which O'Casey finds particularly nauseating, as exemplified by "th' piercin' pipin' of th' rosary be Bing Bang Crosby an' other great film stars, who side-stepped from published greatness for a holy minute or two to send a blessed blast over th' wireless, callin' all Catholics to perpetuatin' prayer."

It is with particular regret that O'Casey sees that even the laborers have been affected by the current attitude. It is significant that the two rough fellows rapidly repent of their interest in Loreleen, a point which may be linked to the comment of Paul Blanshard that the Labour Party in Ireland is not to be compared in strength or in purpose to its counterpart in Great Britain, since it is a small party standing for judicial and piecemeal reform, just as proclerical as any party in the Republic.

The narrow sentimental pietism of modern Ireland is merely one of the many features which O'Casey satirizes in these three plays. He sees as equally disastrous the narrow materialism which has developed with the growth of the middle classes whose bourgeois concern with money and respectability is satirized in each play. Sean O'Faolain, in "Ireland After Yeats," points out that the class which came to power and influence after the revolution of 1916–21 was not a laboring class but rather a developing group of *petite bourgeoisie*—middlemen, importers, and small manufacturers who rose to fill the vacuum left by the departing alien middle class. "These men naturally had very little education and could have only slight interest in the intellectuals' fight for liberty of expression. The upshot of it was a holy alliance between the Church, the new businessmen and politicians, all three nationalist-isolationist for, respectively, moral reasons, commercial reasons, politico-patriotic reasons. The intellectuals became a depressed group. Possibly they were infected by the atmosphere around them. When patriotism begins to cash in it is enough to sicken anyone." It is a common criticism of post-1922 Irish society. The class of which O'Faolain speaks can be weakly sentimental over the past, childishly superstitious, and can squabble among themselves, but the one power that deominates their lives is the power of money and the social status which accompanies it. All other considerations which normally exert a strong influence—personal antipathy, clerical domination—are completely swamped by the new moneymania.

O'Casey visualizes his old capitalists as hunting in pairs, and Michael Marthraun and Sailor Mahan, Flagonson and Farrell foreshadow the uneasy relationship of the Binningtons and the McGilligans. They each have slightly different social spheres. Marthraun and his companion are a small farmer and an ex-sailor doing a lucrative trade in peat taken from the bog

which came to the farmer as part of his wife's dowry.
(O'Casey mentions ironically the new dependence of
the Irish on this traditional fuel in *Sunset and Evening Star*.) Flagonson and Farrell (of *Time to Go*)
are in trade; Reiligan is the chief businessman in a
small country town, while with the Binningtons and
McGilligans we move up in the social sphere—they
have achieved glory as Mayor and Deputy Mayor of
Doonavale, also a small country town, and are doing a
profitable but shady business in timber imported from
somewhere behind the Iron Curtain. The differences,
however, are unimportant. The chief significance lies
in the fact that, big or small, these men are preying
upon society and are doing "more harm to Ireland
living than they'll ever do to Ireland dead."

Marthraun's house and garden tell us much about
him. Like the other capitalists he pays an enthusiastic
lip service to the twin ideals of nationalism and religion, so that yellow and white dominate his garden
and the Irish tricolor flutters from a flag pole, in the
same way as Binninton's drawing room shows a picture of Michael Collins (a leading member of the
Free State government, killed in ambush in the civil
war) on the one hand and St. Anthony of Padua on
the other, while over the tavern and general store in
Time to Go a papal flag presents us with the literal
interpretation of the picture drawn by Father Boheroe
at the beginning of this chapter. The houses of each
of the capitalists tell us much about their inhabitants.
The grass around Marthraun's house is significantly
dry, like Reiligan's meadows, and the house itself is in
a deep black shadow.

In the center, a dignified-looking bronze urn holds a
standoffish, cynical-looking evergreen which immediately reminds us of the "portly, metal garden urn"
which "stands pompously on its pedestal, looking a

little embarrassed that its one use is only to stand and not to serve," belonging to Reiligan. This touch of pretentiousness in Marthraun's garden is repeated in the descriptions of the solid vulgarity of the possessions of the Binningtons and McGilligans in *The Drums of Father Ned*. Mahogany is a favorite symbol of O'Casey for the indecent display of wealth, and even as early as the times described in *Pictures in the Hallway*, the second book of the autobiography, dealing with his early twenties, he is sensitive to the display of mahogany, gleaming glass, and glossy furniture in the house of Anthony Dovergull, the smug employer who tried to dock his wages for a trivial offense.[14] His account of Dovergull's ostentation is very similar in atmosphere and details to the descriptions of the houses of Reiligan, Binnington, and McGilligan, and to their equally glossy American counterpart seen in later years when O'Casey visited a wealthy middle-class family in New York and noticed the sparkle of glass and silver, of mahogany and walnut, snowy white table linen, and rich lace.

Mahogany, with its rich dark glow, and all things that glitter with a hard, metallic, or crystalline effect, are for O'Casey symbols of the sumptuous way of life of the upper and middle classes. The drawing room of Reiligan's house contains a brightly polished mahogany table, playing exactly the same role as the pompous mahogany sideboard in Binnington's room; and the bright metal fender, poker, and tongs are common to the rooms of both Reiligan and Binnington. These things, like the metallic shine of Binnington's bronze figures, gilded vases, and golden clock (perhaps a reference to the clock presented by sycophantic employees to Dovergull in the incident mentioned above), bring to mind the hard, metallic quality of the minds of these men, who, like the shopkeepers of *Time to*

Go, are so preoccupied with precious metal in the form of clinking coins. A fine piano, not to be played, merely for ornament, takes pride of place in both drawing rooms, and Father Boheroe and Bernadette are both warned away from the respective instruments. The thick, beige carpet desecrated by the Codger has its exact counterpart in the Binnington household. The general impression, as O'Casey explicitly states, is to be one of an attempt at Irish middle-class pomp and circumstance. Each room has liberal touches of green. In Reiligan's, the dark green upholstery of the mahogany chairs, in Binnington's the emerald green upholstery and thick curtains of green plush tied back with gold cords symbolize in each case the self-righteous, insincere patriotism of the owners.

When capitalists appear, they are easily identified. Marthraun is over sixty, is dressed in black, and carries the almost inevitable gold watch chain across his waistcoat, like the New York host who "surveyed those present with a look of Aha, I'm here, see, while a pudgy hand fiddled and diddled with a fine watch-chain crossing his superior belly."

Mahan, a pleasanter character, is younger though stout. Reiligan is short, stocky, sturdy; he looks older than his fifty-five years, has small piercing, piglike eyes, and wears pretentious formal clothing, even to the point of a tall hat, of which more will be said later. Binnington and McGilligan are fine examples of O'Casey's idea of the flourishing capitalist; both wear touches of ostentatiously patriotic green, with a watch chain, the former displaying also a cross and harp at the end of his Mayoral chain—another reminiscence of the quotation at the beginning of this chapter. Bull Farrell, as a sign of social pretension, wears a high white collar and black tie, as does Flagonson, whose rotund form indicates his state of mind. The capitalists are usually aging men in the fifties or sixties, often with graying hair, either fleshily plump, like Reiligan, or meanly spare, like Marthraun, and are usually associated with signs of self-righteousness and insincere patriotism.

These physical characteristics, of course, merely indicate an attitude of mind, whether of complacent self-righteousness or meanness. The men spend much energy haggling over money. Mahan and Marthraun return to small-minded bickering over finance from time to time, while a similar note is sounded in "big farmer Conroy an' little farmer Cousins still arguin'," of course, about money. The stark contrast between the current attitude and the ideal one of the Widda and Kelly in *Time to Go* is deliberate—the latter are regarded as mad. The meanness and envy of the times is satirically conveyed by Mahan—"there isn't a one who isn't eager to do to others what others would do to him." Farrell and Flagonson eye each other's profits suspiciously, each denying that he has collected much himself. The meanness of the meal offered to the Young Man and the Young Woman and the high price they have to pay for it at Flagonson's Tavern show that the two capitalists in the play act in accordance with Binnington's philosophy of life, that "There's nothin' more in it than gettin' all you can, holdin' what you have, doin' justice to your religious duties, and actin' decent to a neighbour."

The clink of coins rather than the music of Mozart echoes through the real Ireland, and both the Widda Machree and Kelly chant, in reference to the jingle of coins, that "that's how th' harp o' Tara sounds today." In opposing money, Kelly is, according to Conroy, "makin' a mock of all the things we hold so sacred."

Money, O'Casey points out, has a power above all

else in Ireland. We have seen that the overbearing Father Domineer has no power over the usually submissive Mahan when his orders conflict with business interests; the mutual hatred of Binnington and McGilligan loses its force before the claim of money-making, for "business is business" is the echo that resounds through Ireland. Orange-Catholic antipathy is weakened by the linking power of the coin, and the bigoted Binnington sees no incongruity in having dinner with the Orangeman in the interests of a common deal. The power that can even momentarily unite the North and South is mighty; but the power of business is seen even more compellingly when it overcomes the current hostility to communism; Binnington and Skerighan trade with merchants behind the Iron Curtain, but it was all done in a good cause—and "business is business."

Art and literature are no concern of theirs, since there is no prospect of money in either, and Binnington considers the Tostal a waste of time. This materialism is what O'Casey indicated by the big shop in the speech of Father Boheroe. The shamrock on the gable of the big house represents the ideals of the past, to which these people pay an ostentatious and insincere regard. It is occasionally invoked in support of the low money-grubbing of the present day: "Where's th' freedom our poor boys died to get, if a body daren't ask for what he wants for a thing he's sellin'?" Cousins says sentimentally. We have seen how the false nationalism of these people has been indicated in their household furnishings, yet their true philosophy is voiced by Mrs. Binnington: "All that can be done for a dead hero is to put a headstone over his grave, an' leave him there."

National games, music and dances, and language are all very well in talk, but they are rarely put into practice. Binnington's wife tells him that she has never seen him in an Irish dance—and all he knows of Irish (like Boyle) is a greeting. Binnington protests that he contributes much to the upkeep of such things, but his wife claims that while a shilling for Ireland comes out of one pocket, a pound from Ireland slips into the other. Tara's harp has been replaced by the jingle of coins, and the places connected with Ireland's history have long since been allowed to decay, as O'Casey reminds us in *The Green Crow*, where he quotes a letter to the *Irish Press* where the neglect of ancient sites is also stressed.[15] "Sure, man, they're all gone west long ago, an' the whole face o' th' land is pock-marked with their ruins," the Messenger says. The two young travelers are regarded with surprise when they inquire for the Abbey of Balleyrellig and are told "th' whole thing's lost, man, in thickets, brambles, an' briars." They remember ruefully the high ideals of ancient history and contrast them with the mercenary outlook of the present day. The Codger, too, remembers with shame that that "there's a statue of Ireland's hero, Cuchullain, somewhere up in Dublin. Oh, Keelin, Keelin me darling, I'm Irish an' ashamed of it." The old heroes and memories of the past are still, as in *Purple Dust*, representative of the ancient glories of the Irish people; but now they are contrasted, not with the clownish English, but with their own degenerate posterity.

The women are more sensible in certain respects than their husbands, and Mrs. Binnington tries to patch up matters between her husband and the Orangeman Skerighan, but the women have their own absurdities. They are guilty as their husbands in the newly fashionable snobbery that has overtaken the middle class. Sean O'Faolain has pointed out, as we have seen, that the change in Ireland after the revolution was a social one, in which the chief feature was the emergence of the middle class, and O'Casey makes great play of this in the present works and in the later volumes of his autobiography, where he describes the new class of Irishmen "discussing and practising the arts of refinement when making contacts with eminent people, more eminent people, most eminent people" and observes that "the course of the Easter Rising had been betrayed by the commonplace bourgeois class who laid low the concept of the common good and the common task, and were now decorating themselves with the privileges and powers dropped in their flight by the dear, dead men." One of the seekers after respectability asks O'Casey, of all people, for advice on correct etiquette, and is met with the tart reply,

> "Why not ask some of the seventy-seven dead men?"
> "The seventy-seven—what dead men?"
> "The men executed by your Free State Government."
> "Oh, them! I had nothing to do with their executions, anyhow. The dead are dead, and are neither here nor there, now."
> "They are certainly not here," said Sean with some bitterness. "But it seems to me that these men were put to death to afford you the privilege of donning a tall-hat. It won't be long till the gold harp's taken out of the green flag, and a bright, black tall-hat put in its place. The terrible beauty of a tall-hat is born to Ireland" [16]

This is exactly the theme of the three plays under discussion.

In the plays, O'Casey opens his attack in *Cock-a-Doodle Dandy*, in the hilarious top hat episode. Marthraun is willing to spend his money on a top hat for his meeting with the president, and Mahan comments, "Th' whole disthrict'll be paralysed in a spell when your top-hat comes out to meet the president's top-hat, th' two poor things tryin' to keep people from noticin' what's undher them!" The whole incident of the transformation of the top hat is a comment on the new preoccupation with the social niceties which has absorbed the attention of the Irish people. Reiligan appears in a top hat at one moment, while the Binningtons and McGilligans evince much anxiety on details of deportment for the "Reception or President's givin' for important persons in Dublin Castle."

The result of the unwholesome aspects of Irish life described above is shown in the tendency to emigration from the country to the town and from the town abroad, particularly to England and America. John O'Brien pictures Ireland as stricken and dying, with more of her children and their descendants overseas than at home, and Loreleen in exasperation comments, "Is it any wondher that th' girls are fleein' in their tens of thousands from this bewildhered land?" At the end of the play we are confronted with a visual image of this process, with the departure of the three women, followed by the Messenger with his music and gaiety. The Codger's three sons are in America; Daniel and Manus both leave the country after their frustrated love affairs; and in *The Drums of Father Ned*, the Man of the Pike points out the same thing: "Some hop out of Ireland, some just step out of it . . . but they all go." Flagonson's two children want him to settle them in London and his friend agrees that those who are not already gone are going. "There's ne'er a one, lad or lass, in th' disthrict between seventeen an' thirty."

England, the destination of many of these young people, is, according to Flagonson, an opening into a

godless world. It is regarded throughout by the pietistic Irish as the source of all evil, an unknown, sophisti-
cated world which produced Loreleen, representative
of the dark forces, while Manus has been unsatisfactory ever since he served in the English air force.

As usual, however, there are in each play certain
characters, usually young and energetic, who make a
stand against the deadening forces opposed to them.
In *Cock-a-Doodle Dandy* the three women, particularly Loreleen, are associated with youth, gaiety, and
vigor by their bright clothes, fancy dress, and affection
for the Cock, a symbol of the luring vitality of Loreleen herself. As we have seen in *The Bishop's Bonfire*
the forces mustered on the side of life and love fight a
losing battle and are defeated, and the four young
people lose their chance of normal happiness. It is the
lively old Codger rather than the physically young
people who keeps the spirit of gaiety alive, and his
indomitable figure, which surely owes something to
O'Casey's undying admiration of Shaw, passes
through the tragic scene at the end still undaunted
and still singing. In *The Drums of Father Ned*, however, the forces of life revive, and the young people
make a determined stand on behalf of sincerity, art,
freedom, and courage. Their patriotism is sincere; like
O'Casey they are unafraid of old age and death, and
are entirely opposed to the sordid money-grubbing of
their elders.

The reality of this glimmer of hope is spoken by
O'Casey in *The Green Crow*, for, he says, there *are*
brave ones thinking bravely in Ireland's universities
and among the workers, and all "isn't a sing-song
acceptance among the younger clerics." The hope is
only a glimmer though, and O'Casey is not blinded to
the fact that things are still pretty bad. In *Time to
Go*, the two mysterious characters opposing current
materialism are defeated, the miracle of the blossom-

ing tree fades after a few seconds, and they themselves vanish without having accomplished any change in the attitude of the Irish.

The secular forces opposing reactionary narrowness are in the last two plays supported by a newly emerged clergy, an enlightened group who have been foreshadowed by the Brown Priest in *The Star Turns Red*. There is no doubt that O'Casey here is thinking of his early heroes: Dr. McDonald, "a great man gone, and almost forgotten; but not quite forgotten," Dr. Morgan Sheedy, Canon Hayes, and Father O'Flanagan, all of whom he mentions in the dedication of *The Drums of Father Ned*; and Dr. Hickey, "Gael of Gaels."

Father Boheroe is a well-wishing though rather ineffectual figure who looks on helplessly at the destructive effects of the combined forces of Church and State, the Canon, and Reiligan. His views on the contemporary situation are enlightening; he sees the desolation of the countryside and the lives in it, some of his observations shocking the more conventional of his hearers. He tries in vain to console Manus; to urge Foorawn to give up her vow; and to encourage Keelin and Daniel; but the forces against him are too strong and he is reproved by the Canon. Even his defense of the Codger is of little use. In vain he warns that "even our worship is beginning to have the look of the fool's cap and the sound of jester's bells" and that "we are stripping Joseph of his coat of many colours." He leaves the scene with bitter hopelessness: "Don't be too hard on a poor priest unable to work a miracle," he says to Foorawn. There are, however, signs about him of a certain mysticism. He shocks his hearers from time to time with such remarks as "Whisht! Did you hear that sound of rending? . . . The sounds of clawing hands, of pious fools tearing God's good manners into little pieces," and again, to Keelin, "Listen! . . . I heard God laughing, Keelin . . . Laughing at the punch and judy show of Ballyoonagh." As Keelin and Daniel are forced to separate, the room suddenly becomes dark, a cold wind sweeps through it, and when the light comes again it comes only as a depressing dusk. Father Boheroe alone can interpret it: "It was, my child, a long, sad sigh from God." Father Ned, however, triumphantly achieves what the real-life enlightened clerics failed to do; he brings about a renaissance of enlightenment in Ireland. Like the Cock, he is a force rather than a person; he is never seen, only his drums are heard in the distance. He is in no one place and yet he is everywhere, and his appearance, according to the startled Skerighan, is inhuman, with fierce green eyes in a white face, a wild flop of hair flaming like a burning bush, surrounded by a clerical collar round an invisible neck.

The formalized behavior of the two saints in *Time to Go* indicates that they too are more than human. The Cock, Father Ned, Widda Machree, and Kelly— each symbolizes the power working in the recognizable human fighters in the cause of life and love. Whether it will in the future be successful is doubtful, in spite of the optimistic tone of *The Drums of Father Ned*, for the withdrawal of this very play from the Dublin 1958 Festival because of the objections of Archbishop McQuaid and the equally significant battle over Tennessee Williams' play *The Rose Tattoo* (recounted by David Krause in *Sean O'Casey: The Man and His Work*) are both an ironical comment on the optimism the play expresses. In the next play, his final word on the subject of modern Ireland, he shows us how the intellectuals became, as Sean O'Faolain said, a depressed group. When the writers of a nation have given in, it would seem there is little hope. Certainly O'Casey's last word is not an optimistic one.

11

The Last Word

The preceding group of plays was intended to show a picture of modern Ireland in which all the contemporary faults of prudery and bigotry rising from the alliance of the Church and State predominated. *Behind the Green Curtains*, published in 1961, is equally critical, but this time is aimed particularly at the writers of Ireland who should be, as Reena expects, the "leaders of Ireland's thought," but in fact cower abjectly behind the green curtains of showy patriotism and are beaten into submission by the Church.

This is the main theme of the play, and is perhaps derived from a mocking episode in *Sunset and Evening Star*, in which Cathleen ni Houlihan, visiting England as a modern young woman, sardonically describes the Irish scene, where

> All our poets, dramatists, an' storytellers, are lyin' day an' night, flat on their bellies, just because a leadin' poet, Patrick Kavanagh, has declared that if only the poets an' writers fling themselves prostrate before God, an' admit their dire disthress, they may be admitted into a new dispunsensation; for, said he, all the great poets, says he, were, an' are, those who lie prostrate before God. Before God, it's terrible over there, I'm tellin' yous, gentlemen.[1]

This is in fact the picture presented by O'Casey in the present play. False nationalism and false pietism are the dominant enthusiasms in the Irish scene. The play opens with the view of a house, the top story of which is covered with yellow and white bunting, and ironically displays the green decorated picture of Parnell, whom the clerics helped to ruin.

The date of the play is soon indicated by the mention of the meeting and demonstration for Cardinal Mindszenty, a subject of discussion throughout the play. The imprisonment of the Hungarian Cardinal by the Russians in February, 1949, gave rise to bitter feeling throughout the Church, and the march which causes the group of writers such indecision is a demonstration against this act of violence. In their humble position behind the Legion of Mary they are to carry the banner inscribed, "Free Thought in a Free World," an ironic comment on the restriction of speech and thought imposed on them by the Church; while by the title of the play O'Casey means to imply that the true concern of right-thinking Irishmen is not whatever may happen behind the Iron Curtain of Russia, but behind the equally impenetrable green curtains of Ireland. In a letter to the *Irish Times* he pointed out that "Eire is now, in fact, in the condition of control of thought so often attributed to the socialism of the U. S. S. R." [2]

The power and superstition of the Church are among the subjects under discussion. The comic hagiology of Lizzie and Angela, who are on familiar terms with "Blesseds" as well as saints, is a starting point for satiric comments which continue in the fierce discussion between Beoman the Communist and Basawn the Catholic, in which is heard an echo of O'Casey's former ridicule of the veneration of Lourdes. Fatima and Knock are also mentioned, but the argument centers chiefly around the Weeping Statue of Syracuse.

The superstitious aspects of Catholicism, however,

are a minor threat in comparison with the real and menacing power of the Church, which in this play looms as darkly as in *The Star Turns Red* and in *Cock-a-Doodle Dandy*, where religious beliefs are enforced with brutality. No priest is represented in the play, but the power of religion is represented by the salacious and sadistic fanatic Kornavaun, the prefect of a sodality. He is faintly reminiscent of Rankin and Joybell, in that his pietism is a cover for repressed sexuality, as is shown in his outbursts to Noneen; and in his fanatical witch-hunting there is more than a hint of sadism. It is he who persuades factory workers to come out on strike in protest against a mixed marriage, and he is implicated in the abduction of Chatastray and Noneen, an episode foreshadowed in *Sunset and Evening Star*, in which O'Casey describes the treatment of a farmer and a girl who lived with him as his housekeeper at the hands of the local pietists.[3]

The power which Koranvaun represents is immediately evident. The wavering writers are on the point of entering a Protestant church for the funeral ceremony of a fellow playwright when Kornavaun comes in with the news that attendance of the funeral has been forbidden, and they immediately obey him. Reena, who alone disregards the order, is penalized later for her disobedience. In much the same way O'Casey describes in *The Green Crow* how a football match between Ireland and a Communist nation, Yugoslavia, was promptly cancelled through the intervention of Archbishop McQuaid.[4] The writers return in sackcloth from an interview with the Bishop thoroughly indoctrinated with pietistic ideas, repentant for having shown signs of wavering against Church authority: "We know now that we have to be careful not to include a word in our writin' that might arouse any sinful desire."

Such is the power of the Church in modern Ireland —obscurantist, superstitious, and at times brutal. It is a picture that has been presented in many of the previous plays. It is shown here operating upon one group in particular—the writers and artists of contemporary Ireland. In this play the group is a sorry fellowship. McGeera the dramatist, Horawn the poet, Conneen the actor, and McGeelish, a gossip-writer, are all seen wavering miserably over the question of attending the funeral in the first scene, and are later presented in detail when they visit Senator Chatastray to discuss whether or not to take part in the march of protest. They bicker maliciously among themselves, show petty rivalry for membership in the Irish Academy of Letters, and though they speak boldly enough behind the protecting green curtains they are terrified of Kornavaun and the power he represents and hurry out as soon as his name is mentioned. Their fear is shown too in their ready submission to the Bishop and adoption of his advice. In any case, artistically they are of little use. Horawn's poetic philosophy is a withdrawal into an ivory tower away from the realities of life, and his poetry is very poor stuff. They squabble endlessly among themselves and pry into the private concerns of Chatastray during his absence in a way which bears witness to his later comment, "Ireland's full of squinting probers," and are virtuously shocked to find among his possessions a photograph of "The Maja" and a copy of Renan's controversial *Life of Jesus*. His efforts to free them from clerical domination are in vain; he himself is helpless to save Noneen, and finally he capitulates at the end of the play.

His sitting room tells us much about him. It is "safely furnished," the fire, glasses, and mahogany table giving a touch of self-satisfied opulence. His photograph, which stands on the latter, is flanked by a

vase in which there are no flowers, significantly indicating his lack of appreciation for the finer things of
life. The theme of church domination is once again
indicated by a spire seen through the window, while
the windows themselves display a black clock with
golden hands circled with green and the cross of St.
Patrick, signifying, according to Kornavaun, that he is
"serving God and man"—in other words he is a wav-
erer. Other details of the room are less obviously symbolic. By the Abbey poster we are reminded of the
great days of the Irish theater, once the domain of
Yeats, also a senator, but now patronized by such as
Dennis Chatastray.[5]

The case of books in Gaelic is also an ironic gibe,
for McGeelish later remarks that they are as "clean as
a new pin" and that their owner has only a couple of
words in the national language to which he pays
mouth honor—we have seen before how the attitude
of a man to Gaelic is often used as a touchstone. The
pictures with their whitewashed cottages and picturesque scenes indicate the sentimental nature of his
patriotism, while his pietism is underlined by "a holy
picture of some saint or other to keep Paul Henry
company." The green curtains of the title figure prom-
inently and serve a double purpose. They are green,
and hence serve to put up a front of orthodox patriotism to the world, and at the same time they "blind
some of the squinting eyes."

The symbolic nature of the curtains is emphasized
by the ritualistic dialogue of the writers and by the
rather labored symbolism of Reena's action in drawing aside the curtains "to let th' old air out," indicating that O'Casey had read his Ibsen. The independent
thoughts of the writers are voiced only in the safe
privacy provided by the curtains which screen them
from the outside; Reena, in pulling them back, hopes
to let thoughts escape "into th' cool air of life," and to

let Chatastray hear the "tramp of people's feet," for "when you shut out th' people you are shutting out God." She fails to instill any courage into him, however, and as she leaves the room for the last time the curtains are once more closed across the window, indicating that Ireland will remain shut off from the larger world outside, and Chatastray has joined his friends outside, wearing his yellow and white sash to march in the procession.

The leader of the resistance is as usual a Communist worker—here Beoman, who engages in a derisive debate on miracles in the manner of the Atheist and many other argumentative predecessors of earlier plays, staunchly ejects Kornavaun, who attempts to interfere in factory matters, makes a heroic resistance to the thugs who attempt to abduct Noneen, and is always to be relied upon for the sardonic comment at the appropriate moment. In the end he escorts Noneen to England, and literally carries off Reena, now converted from the Legion of Mary to a more enlightened view. He, Reena, and Noneen are the bulwarks of common sense against the flood of hypocrisy that threatens Ireland; but significantly they, like Lorna, Loreleen, and many others, retreat to England, leaving the field to the victorious pietists and tamed writers.

In addition to his major plays, O'Casey from time to time published a number of one-act plays, some merely amusing and with no relevance to the present study, others of a certain political and social interest. One of these, *Time to Go*, has been considered alongside the three plays dealt with in the previous chapter; other significant playlets are *Figuro in the Night* and *The Moon Shines on Kylenamoe*, both published together with *Behind the Green Curtains*, and an earlier play, *Hall of Healing*.

The first of these, *Figuro in the Night*, is a commentary on the prudery and sex repression of modern Ireland, and is dedicated to a Hungarian postage stamp on which appeared a picture of the statue in the Grand' Place of Brussels representing a small boy in a natural but indiscreet position. It is dedicated also to "the Ferocious Chastity of Ireland." The folk song "Oh, Dear, What Can the Matter Be?" is used as a theme song throughout the play, and the blue ribbons are used as a symbol of youth, joy, and sexual indulgence. It is sung first by the young girl, who, while looking out of the window, comments on the bleakness of the scene and (with an echo of *The Silver Tassie*) the premature death of the young soldiers, commemorated by the Celtic cross for those who died for Ireland and by the obelisk for those who died in the Great War, all of whom died too young to know the joys of love.

While the young die, the old survive; sterile and childless, the old woman and man stumble in, mumbling of their wasted lives. O'Casey's own quotations at the beginning of the play serve as texts for the scene he depicts, telling of the collections of old maids and bachelors in Ireland and the unreasonable puritanism that is forced on the young.

Scene two is reminiscent in many ways of the miraculous scenes of *Cock-a-Doodle Dandy*. The scene has brightened and is flooded with color; the mysterious Figuro has appeared in O'Connell Street and his erotic influence has pervaded the whole crowd. The cries of many birds are heard (Aengus, god of love in Celtic mythology, walked with birds swooping around him), and a birdlike lad, suggesting a crow, with a green cap on his head (The old Green Crow himself, perhaps?) appears to announce the triumph of the Figuro, while the Young Man announces with a good deal of meaning that he has brought home for the

Young Girl the highly symbolic blue ribbons. A dance of young people concludes the play as the Old Men sink down upon the cross and obelisk, symbolic of death, and voices in the distance sing the theme song. The play, with its fantastic theme and celebration of the triumph of youth and sex, is very close to *Cock-a-Doodle Dandy* and *Within the Gates*.

The last play in the book, *The Moon Shines on Kylenamoe*, is reminiscent of *Purple Dust* in its theme. The tiny village in a valley consists of fifteen houses and the little general store that supplies the immediate wants of the people. The appearance of Lord Leslieson of Ottery St. Oswald is the signal for the favorite sport of the Irish, teasing the English, as in *Purple Dust*, here practiced by the railway official, the train driver, the Boy and Girl, and Martha and Cornelius Conroy, who emerge from the house on the right. The Irish squabble among themselves, criticize the courting couple, and obstruct all the Englishman's attempts to get any sense out of them. He demands to be taken to the post office, where there is a telephone, but needless to say this is not possible, and we remember Poges's similar difficulties in establishing communications in *Purple Dust*. He is left at last desolate at the station as the train departs half an hour late, but a hope of better Anglo-Irish relations is seen as Cornelius invites him into his home for the night, offering him the necessary transport for his journey on the morrow. Mrs. Conroy, "a matronly figure in . . . the warm, golden glow flooding from the cosy, sheltering home," seconds the invitation; the Englishman, much moved, is voluntarily made welcome in an Irish home —a great improvement since the days of Stoke and Poges.

The last one-act play mentioned above, *The Hall of Healing*, is a commentary on the state of public health services in Dublin during O'Casey's youth. He himself had suffered much from the inefficiency or heartlessness of doctors who had little sympathy for the poor, and he remembers in his autobiography the bitter time of his mother's death when the doctor refused to prescribe before receiving his fee.

His most vivid experience, however, is detailed in the chapter of the first volume (*I Knock at the Door*), headed "Hill of Healing," in which he describes a visit paid to the outpatient department of a big hospital to have his eyes treated. The visit was to be the first of many, for he suffered throughout his childhood from a painful eye disease, and during these hospital visits he must have observed his surroundings keenly, for he depicts with great accuracy the atmosphere of an outpatient department, with its long rows of waiting people, hard benches, gossip over ailments, and posters descriptive of disease. The treatment he received during the episode he describes seems to have been fair and thorough, for the examination lasted for two hours and the doctor behaved with reasonable consideration for the child and his mother.

Lady Gregory also recounts a conversation with a nursing sister who recalled a visit of O'Casey, at about the time of rehearsal of *The Shadow of a Gunman*, to the dispensary of a Dublin hospital for some remedy for his eyes. He was annoyed when a poor woman came in for some medicine and the sister refused her snappishly because she had brought no bottle. He and the sister went to the store at his suggestion, and they found one for the woman. Later O'Casey sent £2 for the dispensary.

These details are utilized in *The Hall of Healing*, modified, however, to emphasize the cold indifference of the doctor and the sufferings of the poor who attend the dispensary, so that the play, ending with

the death of Red Muffler's child, becomes an indictment of a society which can allow such things. We
remember too, the moving account in the autobiography of how a brother, born to his parents before
O'Casey and given the name he was later to have, died
in his mother's arms at the hospital through the slow-
ness and neglect of the nurses.

The dispensary, unlike the one in the autobiography, which seemed clean enough and boasted a warm
stove, is ugly and none too clean. The patients are
bullied by the doctor, who is suffering from his indul-
gences of the previous night, and by his subservient
assistant, "Alleluia," otherwise Aloysius, the caretaker,
who gives an opportunity for some of O'Casey's favorite satire against petty tyranny and officious piety. He
bullies the patients unmercifully, yet demands their
pennies for "Holy Souls" and piously chants "Alleluia" when the organ is heard playing in the church
next door.

An interesting sidelight is thrown on the play by
O'Casey himself toward the end of the autobiography
in which he refutes the criticisms of a certain Patrick
Galvin, who somewhat officiously charges him with
having exaggerated the picture he draws in the little
play.[6] While agreeing that the play when written had
been based on memories of his youth in Dublin fifty
years ago, O'Casey refers his critic to his own letter to
the *Irish Times* of December 28, 1951, in which he
exclaims, "Little did I think when I wrote *The Hall of
Healing* that the conditions of fifty years ago in the
dispensaries of the poor would be the same today."
Dr. Browne's Mother and Child Bill, introduced in
the hope of alleviating the conditions of working-class
women in Dublin, was at that time being contested in
the Dail, where, by the power of the Hierarchy, who
resented the interference of the state in such matters,

it was shortly rejected. O'Casey points out that letters and articles called forth by the controversy indicated that things were still as bad as ever and that the notorious Red Ticket system, by which paupers were singled out, was still in action at that time.

He notes that on August 5, 1953, a new dispensary was about to be built in County Cavan for £1,000 and asks derisively, "Are they building there a small cabin of clay and wattles made? How much would it cost if it was being built for the care of the soul and the vanity of clerics?" Thus, while admitting that the play was written with memories of a time when he and his mother, like the old woman in the play, had to live on five shillings a week, O'Casey is at pains to point out that, like his other Irish plays, it has a direct reference to conditions and events of the present day which have unhappily altered little since his own youth.

This work concludes the list of O'Casey's published plays. Though a minor, one-act playlet, it is significant that here as throughout all his other work his preoccupation is principally with the plight of ordinary people, a concern which shows itself now in the depiction of slum conditions in Dublin in his early plays, now in the expressionistic revelation of human suffering in war and peace, now in the fight against fascism, now in the struggle to uphold his intensely personal religious conviction of the sacredness of all those qualities—vigor, youth, joy, freedom—which can make the life of the ordinary human so much richer. His profound and urgent belief in the sacredness and beauty of human life is the motivating force behind all his work; it is a belief he has defended more valiantly than any writer of his time. It is upon the validity of his personal beliefs and his fierce integrity in expressing them that O'Casey's claim to greatness rests.

Notes

1—The Rising

1. James Stephens, *The Insurrection in Dublin* (Dublin, 1916).
2. Sean O'Casey, *Mirror in My House* (New York, 1956). This is O'Casey's autobiography. It incorporates in two volumes the autobiography's six books, first published separately (*I Knock at the Door, Pictures in the Hallway, Drums under the Windows, Inishfallen, Fare Thee Well, Rose and Crown,* and *Sunset and Evening Star*). They remain separately paginated in this edition.

2—The Terror

1. Michael O'Maolain, "An Ruathar Ud Agus A nDeachaigh Leis," *Feasta* (May, 1955).

3—Civil War

1. Sean O'Casey, *Inishfallen, Fare Thee Well*, p. 128.
2. *Ibid.*, p. 142.
3. *Ibid.*, p. 159.
4. *Lady Gregory's Journals*, ed. Lennox Robinson (New York, 1947), p. 179.
5. *Ibid.*, p. 195.
6. *Inishfallen*, p. 161.
7. *Irish Independent* (Dublin), October 21, 1913.
8. James Connolly, *Labour in Ireland* (Dublin, 1951), p. 222.
9. *Inishfallen*, pp. 97–98.
10. Arland Ussher, as quoted in Paul Blanshard, *The Irish and Catholic Power* (Boston, 1953), p. 174.

4–The Great War

1. Sir Winston Churchill, *The World Crisis* (London, 1960), p. 8.
2. James Connolly, *Labour and Easter Week* (Dublin, 1949), pp. 51, 44, 28.
3. Churchill, p. 184.
4. Sean O'Casey, *Drums under the Windows*, p. 277.
5. Churchill, p. 8.

5–The Depression

1. Sean O'Casey, *Rose and Crown*, p. 160.
2. Sean O'Casey, *The Green Crow* (New York, 1956), pp. 86–109.

6–The Rise of the Fascists

1. Sean O'Casey, *Sunset and Evening Star*, p. 134.
2. W. P. Ryan, *The Pope's Green Island* (London, 1912), p. 278.

7–The Second World War

1. *The Letters of W. B. Yeats*, ed. Allan Wade (London, 1954), pp. 740–41.

8–Back to Ireland–A Comic Vision

1. Edmund J. Murray, "The Key to the Problem," in *The Vanishing Irish*, ed. John A. O'Brien (New York, 1953), p. 72.
2. Sean O'Casey, *Sunset and Evening Star*, p. 167.
3. Jules Koslow, *The Green and the Red* (New York, 1950), p. 77.
4. Sean O'Casey, *Rose and Crown*, p. 219.
5. Paul Blanshard, *The Irish and Catholic Power*, p. 16.
6. Sean O'Casey, *Inishfallen, Fare Thee Well*, pp. 292–96.

9–A Tragic Vision

1. Sean O'Casey, *Pictures in the Hallway*, p. 246.

2. *Ibid.*, pp. 270–73.

3. W. P. Ryan, *The Pope's Green Island*, p. 276.

4. *Irish Independent*, September 1, 1913.

5. Ryan, p. 277.

6. *Pictures in the Hallway*, pp. 336–40.

7. R. M. Fox, *Jim Larkin* (Dublin, 1957), p. 69.

10 – Contemporary Ireland – The Reality

1. John A. O'Brien, "The Vanishing Irish," in *The Vanishing Irish*, p. 13.

2. Sean O'Casey, *Inishfallen, Fare Thee Well*, p. 216.

3. Paul Blanshard, *The Irish and Catholic Power*, pp. 4–6.

4. *Ibid.*, p. 295.

5. *Inishfallen*, p. 377.

6. Sean O'Casey, *The Green Crow*, p. 138.

7. Sean O'Casey, *Sunset and Evening Star*, pp. 166–67. An interesting and depressing example of the present attitude of Ireland, directed by the clergy, toward the arts and drama in particular was the incident of the Tostal of 1958. The two highlights of the Festival were withdrawn owing to the hostility of Dr. McQuaid, Archbishop of Dublin, who objected to them. They were *The Drums of Father Ned* and Alan McClelland's *Bloomsday*, a dramatic version of James Joyce's *Ulysses*. A full account of the incident is given in David Krause's *Sean O'Casey: The Man and His Work* (London, 1960), pp. 212–17. Dr. Krause also recounts the equally significant battle over Tennessee Williams' *The Rose Tattoo*, pp. 217–21.

8. W. P. Ryan, *The Pope's Green Island*, p. 80.

9. *Inishfallen*, p. 377.

10. Maura Laverty, "Woman-shy Irishmen," in *The Vanishing Irish*, p. 54.

11. Ryan, p. 21.

12. Arland Ussher, "The Boundary between the Sexes," in *The Vanishing Irish*, p. 162.

13. *Inishfallen*, p. 330.

14. Sean O'Casey, *Pictures in the Hallway*, p. 180.

15. *The Green Crow*, pp. 148–49.

16. *Inishfallen*, pp. 208–9.

11 — The Last Word

1. Sean O'Casey, *Sunset and Evening Star*, pp. 150–51.
2. *Irish Times*, August 11, 1944.
3. *Sunset and Evening Star*, p. 310.
4. Sean O'Casey, *The Green Crow*, p. 146.
5. For a comprehensive account of the depressing state of the government-subsidized Abbey Theatre in recent times, see David Krause, *Sean O'Casey: The Man and His Work*, pp. 310–12.
6. *Sunset and Evening Star*, pp. 316–20.

Index